A Christı

MW01030140

Book by

JOSEPH ROBINETTE

Music and lyrics by

BENJ PASEK and JUSTIN PAUL

Based upon the motion picture
A Christmas Story
Distributed by Warner Bros.,
Written by Jean Shepherd, Leigh Brown and Bob Clark
and upon
In God We Trust: All Others Pay Cash
Written by Jean Shepherd

Dramatic Publishing Company
Woodstock, Illinois • Australia • New Zealand • South Africa

©MMXV
Book by JOSEPH ROBINETTE
Music and lyrics by BENJ PASEK and JUSTIN PAUL

Based upon the motion picture
A Christmas Story
Distributed by Warner Bros.,
Written by Jean Shepherd, Leigh Brown and Bob Clark
and upon
In God We Trust: All Others Pay Cash
Written by Jean Shepherd

Printed in the United States of America
All Rights Reserved
(A CHRISTMAS STORY, THE MUSICAL)

ISBN: 978-1-58342-408-7

IMPORTANT BILLING AND CREDIT REQUIREMENTS

A Christmas Story, The Musical had its premier Broadway production at the Lunt-Fontanne Theatre in New York under the direction of James M. Nederlander and James L. Nederlander with opening previews on November 5, 2012. Opening night was held on November 19, 2012, running until December 30, 2012.

Cast (in order of appearance)

Jean Shepherd	Dan Lauria
Ralphie	Johnny Rabe
Ralphie (at certain performances)	Joe West
Mother	Erin Dilly
Randy	Zac Ballard
The Old Man	John Bolton
The Bumpus Hounds	Pete and Lily
Schwartz	J.D. Rodriguez
Flick	Jeremy Shinder
Esther Jane	Analise Scarpaci
Mary Beth	Alexa Niziak
Scut Farkus	Jack Mastrianni
Grover Dill	John Babbo
Other Children	Grace Capeless, Sarah Min-Kyung Park, Luke Spring
Miss Shields	Caroline O'Connor
Fantasy Villian	Mark Ledbetter
Bank Manager	Luke Spring
Bank Robbers	Nick Gaswirth, Thay Floyd
Prisoner	Eddie Korbich
Can-Can Girlfriend	Alexa Niziak
Delivery Men	Thay Floyd, Mark Ledbetter
Mrs. Schwartz	Kirsten Wyatt
Policeman	Mark Ledbetter
Fireman	Thay Floyd
Doctor	Eddie Korbich
Nurse	Kirsten Wyatt
Flick's Mother	Lindsay O'Neil
Mobster Tap Specialty	Luke Spring
Santa Claus	Eddie Korbich
Chief Elves	Andrew Cristi, Kirsten Wyatt
Nancy	Grace Capeless
Goggles Kid	John Babbo
Waiter	Andrew Cristi
Waitress	Sarah Min-Kyung Park

Cast (continued)

Neighbors, Shoppers, Parents, Students,
Townspeople, Elves & Others..........................Tia Altinay, John Babbo,
Charissa Bertels, Grace Capeless,
Andrew Cristi, Thay Floyd, Nick Gaswirth,
Eddie Korbich, Mark Ledbetter, Jose Luaces,
Jack Matrianni, Alexa Niziak, Lindsay O'Neil,
Sarah Min-Kyung Park, J.D. Rodriguez,
Analise Scarpaci, Lara Seibert, Jeremy Shinder,
Luke Spring, Kirsten Wyatt

Production Staff

Director ....John Rando
Producers..Gerald Goehring, Roy Miller,
Michael F. Mitri, Pat Flicker Addiss,
Peter Billingsley, Timothy Laczynski,
Mariano Tolentino Jr., Louise H. Beard,
Michael Filerman, Scott Hart, Alison Eckert,
Bob Bartner, Michael Jenkins,
Angela Milonas, Bradford W. Smith
Associate Producers...Vincent G. Palumbo,
Dancap Productions, Inc.,
Jeffrey Jackson, Ric Zivic
Casting ....Stephanie Klapper, CSA
Music Coordinator .... Talitha Fehr
Choreographer.. Warren Carlyle
Associate Choreographer...James Gray
Dance music arrangements .... Glen Kelly
Vocal arrangements... Justin Paul
Orchestrations .... Larry Blank
Music direction & supervision...................................... Ian Eisendrath
Production Stage Manager...Peter Wolf
Technical Supervisor... Fred Gallo
General management ....Corker Group, LLC, John S. Corker
Press Representative ....Keith Sherman & Associates
Advertising & marketing .... aka
Set design... Walt Spangler
Costume design..Elizabeth Hope Clancy
Lighting design .... Howell Binkley
Sound design.. Ken Travis
Hair & wig design..Tom Watson
Animals trained by...William Berloni

The world premiere of *A Christmas Story, The Musical* was produced by Kansas City Repertory Theatre with Eric Rosen, artistic director, Jerry Genochio, producing director, and Cynthia Rider, managing director.

Subsequently produced by The 5th Avenue Theatre, Seattle, Wash., with David Armstrong, executive producer and artistic director, Bernadine C. Griffin, managing director, and Billy Berry, producing director.

A Christmas Story, The Musical

CHARACTERS

JEAN SHEPHERD/NARRATOR: Late 40s to early 60s. A charismatic storyteller who has the ability to weave a spell and draw an audience into his magical world. He is omniscient but not overpowering—a good-natured curmudgeon with a deadpan sense of humor. He holds the audience with his tremendous presence and spark. [Note: The framing device begins with Jean's radio show, but as the action unfolds he becomes a physical part of the storytelling, a narrator who comes in and out of the scenes. When he is onstage as the narrator, he is unnoticed by the other characters (except for the few occasions when he has direct interaction with Ralphie). When Jean assumes an onstage role (e.g., the telegram deliverer), he is, of course, seen by the others as that character. When Jean is observing Ralphie, he feels and expresses everything just as Ralphie would, exactly paralleling the boy's emotional state. The "Universal I" phrase that Jean uses in his opening speech is his way of distancing himself from the story, but it is truly autobiographical in nature.]

THE PARKERS:

RALPHIE: 9, going on 10 (may be played by a 9 to 12-year-old). Cute and winsome, but not precious. Bright, but not precocious. A regular kid you wouldn't mind having as a next-door neighbor. He's a bit mischievous and rascally but with a twinkle in his eye.

MOTHER: 30s to 40s. More in charge of the family than the Old Man is, but she would never let him know it. She is warm and affable … at times a bit daffy … but not a pushover. A vibrant woman, she is always busy, especially anytime she's in the kitchen. She is the secret engine that keeps the family running, keeping the household together with an impressive balancing act.

THE OLD MAN: 30s to 40s. A guy with a good heart, though it is buried beneath a sometimes gruff (and rough) exterior. He's a devoted husband and father who loves his family but doesn't overtly show it. He usually expects the worst but is capable of excitement if the situation warrants (though it usually doesn't). In his moments of fantasy, he is transformed from his usual grumbling blue-collar self to a true song and dance man.

RANDY: 7 to 8 (may be played by a 7 to 10-year-old). Ralphie's younger brother. Cute, cuddly and whiny. Admires Ralphie but won't admit it. He's at the stage of childhood wherein he seems opposed to everything, but he's still lovable—not a brat.

THE KIDS *(may be doubled)*:

SCHWARTZ: a classmate.

FLICK: a classmate.

ESTHER JANE: a classmate.

MARY BETH: a classmate.

SCUT FARKUS: 14 to 15. The textbook example of a schoolyard bully, except this truant doesn't go to school. He is loud, obnoxious and intimidating. Older than Ralphie and his classmates by a year or two, he wears a perpetual scowl beneath his trademark coonskin cap. He always appears at the most inopportune times to scare and harass his innocent victims.

GROVER DILL: 9 to 12. Always at Farkus' side is his toady, Dill. Much younger and decidedly smaller than Farkus, Dill delights in being tethered to his "hero." He punctuates the bully's threats and warnings with a series of rapid-fire belly-laughs, thus making the two of them the scourge of the neighborhood whenever they appear. But, like most of their ilk, when the two are finally challenged and bested, they turn out to be the biggest cowards of all.

BOY	CUSTOMERS
GIRLS (3)	TAP SPECIALTY BOY
NANCY	GOGGLES KID
BANK TELLERS	WAITER'S DAUGHTER

THE ADULTS (*may be doubled*):

MISS SHIELDS: Mid 30s to late 50s. The local elementary school teacher. A seemingly stereotypical 1940s educator—prim and proper. Stern when necessary, though warm—and even humorous—when the situation merits it. In Ralphie's fantasy, she becomes a dynamic, show-stopping, brassy belter and tapper—a force to be reckoned with.

SANTA: Early 30s to early 60s. The Santa Claus at Higbee's Department Store is decidedly unlike the typical "Jolly Old Elf" of legend and lore. Ill-tempered and slightly inebriated, he is unhappy with his job. He dismisses each child as quickly as possible in an attempt to put an end to the day and, perhaps, head for the nearest "watering hole."

ELVES (8)	CUSTOMERS
DELIVERY MEN (2)	CAN-CAN GIRLS
TOWNSPEOPLE	CAN-CAN GIRLFRIEND
PARENTS	POLICEMAN
VILLAIN	FIREMAN
BANKROBBERS (2)	DOCTOR
ESCAPED PRISONER	NURSE
BARTENDER	WAITER

SETTINGS

ACT I

PROLOGUE: Christmas Eve, several years ago
New York City
A street corner outside the radio studio of Station WOR
The radio studio desk

SCENE 1: December 1, 1940
The Parker family house
Higbee's Department Store

SCENE 2: The next day
The Parker family house
A small portion of the outside yard

SCENE 3: Soon afterward
A path leading to school

SCENE 4: A few minutes later
The classroom

SCENE 5: A week later
The Parker family house

SCENE 6: Early evening on December 13, 1940
The Parker family house

SCENE 7: Immediately following
On the road

SCENE 8: Late that night
The Parker family house

ACT II

MUSICAL NUMBERS - ACT I

MUSICAL NUMBERS - ACT II

PRODUCTION NOTES

FARKUS and DILL: The two villains are not members of Ralphie's class. They are, however, used in production numbers that occur outside of school and, of course, in any scenes where they have lines.

THE BUMPUS HOUNDS: In the original Broadway production, live trained dogs were used to great effect. If trained dogs are not available, it is suggested that adult or child actors might portray the animals or that puppets be used. If not practical, all of The Old Man's lines about—and to—the dogs may be played and delivered offstage before he enters the house and/or through the open door when he comes inside.

BB GUNS: In the simpler times of 1940's America, the wish for a Christmas or birthday BB gun was on many a young person's list. It was a very common gift in those days. Most of the instances of guns being used in this show, particularly by the ensemble, can be done with guns in boxes with a picture on the outside of the box (as appeared on the original Red Ryder box). Only in the fantasy, "Ralphie to the Rescue" and in the final moments of the show—when Ralphie unwraps his gift—do we actually see a real BB gun being held.

A Christmas Story, The Musical

ACT I

(#1: "Overture")

PROLOGUE

(New York City. A street corner outside the radio studio at Station WOR. Christmas Eve, many years ago.

At C is a Salvation Army SANTA, slowly and rhythmically ringing a hand bell next to a donation kettle hanging from a tripod. Anxious shoppers and businesspeople hurry along their way, ignoring SANTA and his bell. Near the end of the "Overture," JEAN SHEPHERD, wearing an overcoat, gloves and hat enters. He stops, tosses a few coins into the kettle and begins to walk toward the suggestion of a radio studio that has materialized, in some form, DC. Perhaps a desk, containing a microphone, which may have an "On Air" sign attached. SANTA gives the bell a good-natured scolding ring, stopping JEAN, who pulls out a couple of bills and ceremoniously drops them into the kettle. As JEAN goes to leave, SANTA once more stops him with a rather violent ringing of the bell. JEAN, incredulous, tosses his remaining change in the bucket. SANTA resumes the rhythmic ringing and disappears from view. JEAN moves to the studio, removes his outer garments, signals to an unseen engineer, sits and speaks into a microphone.)

JEAN *(as the "Overture" ends, delivered with high energy, excitement and a wry, nostalgic sensibility)*. Hi, gang! Are you ready to play radio on this blustery, blizzardy Christmas Eve? I am if you are. Yes, once again, right here on WOR in the heart of Manhattan, it's "The Jean Shepherd Show."

(He blows "Charge!" on a kazoo.) Home of the greatest stories ever told—by yours truly, of course. On my way into the studio, in the spanking December breeze, I passed by a Salvation Army Santa Claus listlessly tolling his bell, and remembered another Christmas, in another time, in another place, and … a gun. I take you back to the exotic city of—*(Anticlimactic.)* Hohman, Indiana—where the state line ends abruptly in the icy, detergent-filled waters of Lake Michigan. Back in the day, Lake Michigan was so polluted you could run halfway to Milwaukee before you sank to the bottom. Any-the-how, it was there in Hohman, back in 1940, that I experienced my most important

(#1a: "Transition to 1940")

JEAN *(cont'd)*. Yuletide season. Now when I say the word "I," I don't mean me, necessarily. It's a universal "I." And the "I" in this particular story is Ralphie Parker. So sit back, turn up the volume and let's go!

(JEAN "orchestrates" the set change as the studio goes off, and the interior of the Parker house comes into view.)

SCENE 1

(The Parker family house and outside. December 1, 1940.)

MOTHER *(impatiently)*. Ralphie!

(Action onstage freezes.)

JEAN. There it is! The house on Cleveland Street.

(#2: "It All Comes Down to Christmas" [Part 1])

MOTHER *(calling upstairs to RALPHIE and RANDY, with growing urgency)*. We have to go right now! I'm not kidding, boys! Do you want to miss it?

(Action onstage freezes.)

JEAN. My mother in the kitchen, trying in vain to get us bundled up and out the door.

MOTHER. Ralphie! Randy! I mean now!!

(RANDY enters from the upstairs, going downstairs, not eager to venture out into the blizzard.)

RANDY. Aw, Mom!

MOTHER. Randy—now!

(Action onstage freezes.)

JEAN. My kid brother Randy—

RANDY *(as MOTHER begins to dress him)*. Awwwwww …

(We see RALPHIE in his bedroom holding a magazine.)

JEAN. And there I am with my December issue of *The Open Road For Boys*, itchingly, nervously, obsessing over a three-colored, framed, full-page back cover advertisement of the greatest gift a boy could ever hunger for—and realizing that time was my enemy.

RALPHIE.
    GOODBYE NOVEMBER
    THANKSGIVING'S GONE
    NOW EV'RY HOUSE YOU PASS
    HAS A PLASTIC REINDEER ON ITS LAWN

MOTHER *(calling to upstairs, snappy)*. Ralphie! Please!

RALPHIE.
    IT'S ALMOST CHRISTMAS
    THAT'S CLEAR TO SEE
    AND THERE'S A CERTAIN SOMETHING
    THAT I WANT BENEATH MY TREE

MOTHER *(calling to offstage)*. Frank! Start the car, the boys are almost ready!

RALPHIE *(starts downstairs)*.
> THIS YEAR
> DON'T WANT ANOTHER PLAID TIE
> THIS YEAR
> CAN'T LET MY CHANCE PASS BY
> AND I'M RUNNING OUT OF TIME!

MOTHER *(fed up)*. Ralphie!

RALPHIE *(eagerly)*.
> THERE'S A GIFT I GOTTA GET
> AND IT ALL COMES DOWN TO CHRISTMAS
> I KNOW THE CLOCK IS SET
> AND IT ALL COMES DOWN TO CHRISTMAS
> I'VE GOT ONE SHOT AND IT'S TWENTY-FOUR DAYS
>   AWAY!
> I HAFTA HURRY UP
> 'CAUSE IT ALL COMES DOWN TO CHRISTMAS DAY!

(MOTHER helps RALPHIE into his coat.

Outside, sounds of the BUMPUS HOUNDS barking are heard as THE OLD MAN enters.)

THE OLD MAN. Get away! Get away! Shoo! Shoo!

JEAN. And then there's my old man—

THE OLD MAN *(disgruntled, this is a daily occurrence)*. Bumpus! Call 'em off. Bumpus!

JEAN. My old man and the Bumpus hounds next door.

THE OLD MAN. Get out of here you rotten—no no no!

(The BUMPUS HOUNDS chase THE OLD MAN across the stage.)

THE OLD MAN *(cont'd)*. Bumpus! Call 'em off!

JEAN. Our neighbors, the Bumpuses, were so low down on the evolutionary chain they weren't even included in Darwin's family tree.

THE OLD MAN *(firing off a series of grumbled fake-swears).* Consarned gadbits cummerbuts rackin' frackin' flick-flockin' sham-shuckin' mangy mutts!

RALPHIE *(cobbling together a plan).*
    I HAVE A MISSION
    I HAVE A PLAN
    I KNOW TO GET THAT GIFT
    I'VE REALLY GOTTA GET TO MY OLD MAN

THE OLD MAN *(entering the house).* Stupid hillbillies!

RALPHIE.
    AND THEN THERE'S MOTHER
    SHE CAN BE TOUGH.
    I'LL DROP A COUPLE HINTS
    MAYBE THAT'LL BE ENOUGH!

(RALPHIE makes an effort to get MOTHER to notice the Red Ryder BB gun advertisement.)

MOTHER. The store windows are lit at six o'clock. You don't want to miss it, do you, boys?

RANDY *(overlapping).* Come on, Ralphie—we got to get to Higbee's!

JEAN *(with nostalgic anticipation).* Ah, Higbee's. The high-water mark of the pre-Christmas season was the corner window at Higbee's Department Store. The window was now packed with gifts galore. Including the gift of my constant yearning.

(RANDY, MOTHER and THE OLD MAN exit outside as the house begins to fly away and the Parkers' car is revealed.)

RALPHIE.
>THIS YEAR
>DON'T WANT A BOOK I WON'T READ
>THIS YEAR
>I KNOW THE THING THAT I NEED
>
>AND I'M—RUNNING OUT OF TIME.

RANDY, MOTHER & THE OLD MAN *(a bit frenetic).*
>TO HIGBEE'S
>THAT WINDOW!
>WE GOTTA GO!

(THE PARKERS are in the car and drive downtown to Higbee's Department Store. Trees swirl by.)

THE PARKERS.
>NOT A SECOND CAN WE SPARE
>'CAUSE IT ALL COMES DOWN TO CHRISTMAS

MOTHER & THE OLD MAN *(exasperated).*
>WE'RE PULLING OUT OUR HAIR
>'CAUSE IT ALL COMES DOWN TO CHRISTMAS

THE PARKERS.
>WE'VE GOT ONE SHOT AND IT'S TWENTY-FOUR DAYS

MOTHER.	RALPHIE & RANDY.	THE OLD MAN.
AWAY	AWAY	
	AWAY	AWAY

THE PARKERS.
>WE HAFTA HURRY UP
>'CAUSE IT ALL COMES DOWN TO CHRISTMAS DAY!

(Music segues to the next song.)

(#2a: "It All Comes Down to Christmas" [Part 2])

(Various children appear, in a dream-like state, filled with deep yearning.)

KIDS (SOPRANO 2).
    THIS YEAR
    I WANT A SHINY RED BIKE

KIDS (ALTO).
    I WANT A MODEL TOY PLANE

KIDS (SOPRANO 1).
    HOW 'BOUT A LIONEL TRAIN!

(Adults appear around them, forming family clusters.)

ENSEMBLE & TOWNSMAN.
    THIS YEAR

TOWNSMAN *(grouchy)*.
    I WANT
    A WIFE WHO CAN COOK

TOWNSWOMEN 1 & 2.
    I WANT MY KID TO EARN A'S

TOWNSMEN 1, 2 & 3.
    I HOPE THEY GIMME THAT RAISE!

ALL KIDS.
    AND I'M RUNNING OUT OF TIME!

THE PARKERS & ADULT ENSEMBLE.
    WE'RE GETTING CLOSE TO CHRISTMAS

ENSEMBLE.	KIDS.
WE'RE GETTING CLOSE TO CHRISTMAS	THERE'S ONLY TWENTY-FOUR DAYS

ENSEMBLE.
    IT ALL COMES DOWN TO CHRISTMAS

ALL.
    TO CHRISTMAS DAY!

(A flurry of activity as parents prepare themselves and their children for the bitter cold outside. Hats, gloves, and scarves abound.)

ENSEMBLE.
>WE'RE SCRIMPING AND WE'RE SAVING
>'CAUSE IT ALL COMES DOWN TO CHRISTMAS

KIDS *(a realization).*
>WE BETTER START BEHAVING
>'CAUSE IT ALL COMES DOWN TO CHRISTMAS

ALL.
>WE'VE GOT ONE SHOT AND IT'S TWENTY-FOUR DAYS

KIDS ENSEMBLE.	TOWNSWOMEN.	TOWNSMEN.
AWAY	AWAY	
		THIRTY-FOUR THOUSAND, FORTY-NINE MINUTES
AWAY		

MEN (TENOR).		
ALMOST CHRISTMAS	ALMOST CHRISTMAS	AWAY

ALL.
>CHRISTMAS DAY!
>*(With determined cheer, they face the storm.)*
>WE'LL BRAVE THE BITTER WEATHER
>'CAUSE IT ALL COMES DOWN TO CHRISTMAS
>AND MAKE IT THROUGII TOGETIIER
>'CAUSE IT ALL COMES DOWN TO CHRISTMAS

ENSEMBLE.
>WE'VE GOT ONE SHOT AND IT'S TWENTY-FOUR
>DAYS AWAY!

ALL.

>TIME IS ALMOST UP
>AND IT ALL COMES DOWN TO CHRISTMAS

SOPRANO 1, TENOR 1 & BARITONE 1.	SOPRANO 2, ALTOS & TENOR 2.	RALPHIE & KIDS.
DAY!	ALMOST CHRISTMAS!	ALMOST CHRISTMAS!
CHRISTMAS DAY!	NEARLY CHRISTMAS DAY!	NEARLY CHRISTMAS DAY!

(On the button of the number, we find the ENSEMBLE and THE PARKERS staring out front, looking through Higbee's store window, which has materialized in front of them.)

(#2b: "Higbee's Window")

(In sudden commotion, all the KIDS and PARENTS exclaim what they see and what they want in the window.)

KID 1. Look. It's Raggedy Ann and Andy!

KID 2. Lincoln Logs! That's what I want!

NANCY'S MOTHER. Nancy, see Mrs. Claus sitting in the rocking chair?

KID 3. Tinkertoys! Tinkertoys!

KID 4. Mama—Daddy, can I have the red wagon?

KID 4'S FATHER. A Radio Flyer. That's expensive, son.

KID 4. Well, can I?

KID 4'S MOTHER. You have to ask Santa, dear.

(Sudden exclamation and joy from all as they survey the window. The music swells in excitement. JEAN appears at C, wearing Red Ryder's outfit and carrying the BB gun. The ENSEMBLE and KIDS freeze.)

RALPHIE *(a burst of excitement, he is coming face-to-face with what, up until now, he has only dreamed about).* That's it! That's it!

JEAN *(as Red Ryder).* Boys, at last you can own …

RALPHIE.
> AN OFFICIAL RED RYDER RANGE MODEL CAR-
> BINE-ACTION BB GUN

ENSEMBLE & KIDS *(as if the gates of heaven have dramatically burst open).*
> AH!

RALPHIE.
> WITH A COMPASS IN THE STOCK
> AND THIS *THING* THAT TELLS TIME

ENSEMBLE & KIDS.
> AH!

(#3: "Red Ryder Carbine-Action BB Gun")

JEAN *(as himself).* The fever was well upon me. For months, I had thought about a Red Ryder air rifle. And now, there it was! The real thing!

RALPHIE *(a slow realization).*
> YOU DON'T NEED A STEED TO BE A COWBOY
> *NO,* YOU'RE NOT A HERO JUST BY
> GALLOPING OFF IN THE SUN
>
> WHAT YOU REALLY NEED TO BE A COWBOY
> FEARLESS, KEEPIN' BANDITS TREMBLIN' ON THE RUN
> IS A RED RYDER CARBINE-ACTION BB GUN

(The ENSEMBLE and KIDS fade away as RALPHIE steps through the window and joins RED RYDER who hands him a box containing the gun.)

JEAN *(as Red Ryder)*. That's right, boys! If you want to keep your homestead free of villains, I give you—OLD BLUE!

RALPHIE. *(fantasizing, concocting scenarios in which he might use the gun)*.
SEE ME STANDING GUARD UP AT MY WINDOW
I'LL PROTECT THE NEIGHBORHOOD SO
OUTLAWS ARE ALWAYS OUTDONE

AND I'LL BOMBARD THEM FROM THAT WINDOW
SHOW THOSE WEASELS HOW THE
WILD WEST WAS WON!
BANG! BANG!
WITH A RED RYDER CARBINE-ACTION BB GUN

MY TEACHER COULD BE TAKEN BY A PACK OF GOONS
MY CLASS MIGHT BE INVADED BY RACCOONS!
THE KIDS WOULD HURRY DOWN THE HALL
AS TIGERS TRY TO EAT THEM ALL
BUT THEY WOULD BE OK
I'D SWOOP IN AND SAVE THE DAY!

AND THE GIRLS WOULD SIGH AND SAY, "OOOH, RALPHIE!"
WHEN YOU'RE BIG AND BRAVE LIKE ME
NO BULLY CAN EVER MAKE FUN
MY MOM IS CRYIN' *"COWBOY RALPHIE"*
WHILE MY DAD IS YELLIN'
"THAT BOY, HE'S MY SON!"
WITH A RED RYDER CARBINE-ACTION BB GUN

(He gets lost in this dream for just a moment, then is quickly snapped back to reality.)

BUT IT'S ALMOST NEARLY GETTING CLOSE
COUNTING DOWN, THE CLOCK IS SET
DON'T KNOW HOW, DON'T KNOW WHO
BUT I JUST KNOW I GOTTA GET
A RED RYDER CARBINE—

JEAN.
>   *A RED RYDER CARBINE!*

RALPHIE.
>   STOCK WITH A COMPASS—

JEAN.
>   *WITH A COMPASS IN THE STOCK!*

RALPHIE *(with triumph)*.
>   RED RYDER CARBINE-ACTION BB GUN!

(#3a: "It All Comes Down to Christmas" [Reprise])

(The ENSEMBLE enters hurriedly, finishing their shopping before bundling up and heading home. RALPHIE's fantasy is over, the Red Ryder BB gun is a million miles away.)

ALL.
>   THE LINES ARE GETTING LONGER
>   'CAUSE IT ALL COMES DOWN TO CHRISTMAS

TOWNSMEN 1 & 2 *(surreptitiously)*.
>   OUR DRINKS ARE GETTING STRONGER
>   'CAUSE IT ALL COMES DOWN TO CHRISTMAS

RALPHIE *(determined desperation)*.
>   I'VE GOT ONE SHOT

ALL.
>   AND IT'S TWENTY-FOUR DAYS AWAY!
>   IT ALL COMES DOWN TO CHRISTMAS DAY!

(As the ENSEMBLE and KIDS exit, the Parker family house reassembles. We hear barking dogs. MOTHER is in the kitchen stirring a pot on the stove. THE OLD MAN sits at the table, flipping through mail.)

SCENE 2

(The Parker family house and a small portion of the outside yard. The next day.)

MOTHER.
THERE'S SO MUCH MORE TO DO
AND IT ALL COMES DOWN TO CHRISTMAS …
(Calling to upstairs.)

Ralphie! Randy! Breakfast! Get ready for school!

(JEAN blows a puff of snow from his hand, creating a snow-fall effect.)

MOTHER *(cont'd)*. Goodness gracious. It's a blizzard already. And December's just begun.

JEAN. With only twenty-three days till zero hour, and my mission already well underway, my father had embarked on a quest of his own.

THE OLD MAN. Bills … bills … bills. Hey, look—here it is! *(Opens an envelope and withdraws a puzzle page. He goes to work on it.)*

JEAN. The Depression days were the golden age of the crossword puzzle. And my old man was hooked. Contest after contest, my old man labored doggedly. He entered them all, but this was the farthest he'd ever gotten.

THE OLD MAN *(struggling, in frustration)*. Argh!

MOTHER. What's wrong, dear?

THE OLD MAN. What is the name of the Lone Ranger's nephew's horse?

MOTHER *(nonchalantly)*. Uh. Victor. His name is Victor.

THE OLD MAN. How did you know that?

MOTHER *(in a matter-of-fact manner)*. Oh, everybody knows that.

THE OLD MAN *(incredulous, muttering)*. "Everybody knows that."

MOTHER. Is that another one of your silly contests?

THE OLD MAN. Silly? You'll see—you'll see! I'll have you know that I received an official notice that I have made the semifinals!! "You could win $50,000 or hundreds of valuable prizes."

(#4: "The Genius on Cleveland Street")

THE OLD MAN *(cont'd)*. I just need to finish, get this in the mail by tomorrow, and I could be a winner.

MOTHER. That's nice, dear. *(Walks away to continue working in the kitchen.)*

THE OLD MAN *(with determined grit and Herculean effort)*.
THE WHEELS IN MY MIND JUST KEEP ON SPINNING
ANOTHER EXHAUSTING CLIMB UPHILL
I ALWAYS COME CLOSE TO ALMOST WINNING
JUST FOCUS AND THINK
I'M PRACTIC'LLY THERE
IF I COULD GET INK
IN EACH LITTLE SQUARE

I'D BE THE GENIUS ON CLEVELAND STREET
(In self-satisfied delight.)
YEAH ...
AN INTELLECTUAL ELITE
(Laughs.)
I COULD WIN AN AWARD
A TROPHY FOR ALL TO SEE
IMAGINE THAT ...
THE GENIUS ON CLEVELAND STREET
THE GUY THE NEIGHBORS WANNA GREET
THAT MENTAL MACHINE
THE GENIUS ON CLEVELAND STREET

(Giving himself a pep talk.)

> I'M BRIMMING WITH BRAINS AND SKILL AND
>   KNOWLEDGE
> I'M HARDLY A HUMDRUM AVERAGE JOE
> SO I DIDN'T COME FROM SOME DUMB COLLEGE
>
> BUT IF THIS COULD WORK
> WELL, THEN I COULD GO
> FROM "PARKER THE JERK"
> TO "PARKER THE PRO"
>
> *OH,* I'D BE THE GENIUS ON CLEVELAND STREET
> THE CRACKERJACK THAT CAN'T BE BEAT
> SO SMART IT'S OBSCENE!
> THE GENIUS ON CLEVELAND STREET

Two more to go …

> *"DANISH PRINCE THAT SHAKESPEARE PENNED*
> *STABBED AND POISONED IN THE END"*

(MOTHER takes a canned ham clearly labeled "HAM" from the cupboard and sets it on the counter.)

THE OLD MAN *(cont'd).*

> *HAMLET! HA!*
>
> *"CAPTAIN HOOK, HE MUST DESTROY*
> *TINKERBELL'S PAL, FOREVER A BOY"*
> *P-E-T-E-R …*

Three more letters. Peter … Peter…

(MOTHER bangs on a pan, THE OLD MAN doesn't get the hint. She tries to supply him with the answer without damaging his delicate ego.)

THE OLD MAN *(cont'd).* Peter … *(Bang!)* Peter … *(Bang!)* Peter … the wolf. Peter the Great. Peter … Piper picked a peck of pickled peppers. Doesn't fit.

(MOTHER's banging becomes more incessant.)

THE OLD MAN *(cont'd)*. Peter … Peter … Peter … Saint Peter … Saint Petersburg … Peter Rabbit?! *(To MOTHER.) Hey!*

(Music out. MOTHER ceases her banging.)

THE OLD MAN *(cont'd)*. I'm trying to think!

(A beat.)

THE OLD MAN *(cont'd, casually)*. Oh, Peter Pan.
    MISTER PARKER, YOU'RE THE BEST
    NO QUESTION YOU'RE THE BEST WE'VE EVER SEEN!

    WHAT A GENIUS ON CLEVELAND STREET

MOTHER *(sweetly, playing along, letting him believe it)*.
    THE GENIUS ON CLEVELAND STREET

THE OLD MAN.
    THE WHIZ WHOSE PUZZLE IS COMPLETE!

MOTHER.
    IT'S SOMEHOW COMPLETE

THE OLD MAN.
    IF I SEND IT IN
    AND SOMEHOW I WIN, THEY'LL SEE

(He finishes his puzzle and slips it into an envelope, preparing to mail it.)

THE OLD MAN.
    I'M THE GENIUS ON CLEVELAND STREET!

MOTHER.
    THE GENIUS ON CLEVELAND STREET

THE OLD MAN.
>WHO WON'T GO DOWN IN DEFEAT

(A dream is within reach.)

>*LET THIS BE IT!*
>*LET THIS BE THE ONE*
>FOR THE GENIUS ON CLEVELAND STREET!

(THE OLD MAN licks and seals his envelope, placing it in the mailbox on the button of the song. We then hear barking as the BUMPUS HOUNDS chase THE OLD MAN away once again.)

THE OLD MAN *(cont'd)*. No, no, no, Bumpus! Call 'em off! Call 'em off!

(We refocus inside the Parker house.)

MOTHER *(calling upstairs)*. Boys, breakfast! Hurry. You'll both be late for school.

RALPHIE *(coming down the stairs, engaging in a recurring argument)*. Get out of my way, Randy!

RANDY. You get out of my way, Ralphie.

RALPHIE. I was here first.

(RALPHIE and RANDY take their seats at the kitchen table as they jostle each other.)

RANDY. Was not!

RALPHIE. Was too!

RANDY. Was not!

RALPHIE. Was too!

RANDY. Was not!

RALPHIE. Was too!

RANDY. Was not!

RALPHIE. Was too!

THE OLD MAN *(growls)*. Shut up!

MOTHER. Hurry up now and eat.

(Just as they take their seats to eat, a loud boom is heard beneath the kitchen. A puff of smoke billows out of the furnace grate.)

THE OLD MAN. What was that?

MOTHER *(they both know all too well)*. It sounded like the furnace again, dear.

THE OLD MAN *(slowly unleashing his rage)*. It's the clinkers … It's the consarned, goobly-degooking, racklin'ash! *(Goes toward the door to the cellar.)* Sons britches motor-floggin' cake-sniffin' shirty plastards!

(He exits down into the furnace room, continuing the faux profanity as MOTHER covers RANDY's ears.)

THE OLD MAN *(cont'd)*. Farfangled britches, cobbler-goblin'.

(Continues to ad-lib faux profanity until he is heard falling, accompanied by a crash.)

THE OLD MAN *(cont'd, yelling from the basement)*. Who left the skates on the steps!?

(#4a: "The Furnace Blues")

JEAN *(with an air of pride)*. My old man was one of the most feared furnace fighters in northern Indiana. He had lots of practice. And the blue streak coming out of his mouth was equal to the blue smoke pouring out of the furnace grate.

THE OLD MAN. Who turned the damper down?! You *have* to leave it up! Clinkers again. Cob-globbering, tuttin-fruitten clinkers.

(He continues faux-swearing and banging around downstairs. We then hear the sound of footsteps climbing the stairs. THE OLD MAN re-enters, covered in soot.)

THE OLD MAN *(cont'd)*. The fufaluckin' fumulgatin', faarfignugin flopchockitty furnace has gone out again. *(To MOTHER.)* Call the office and tell them I'll be late. *(He exits down the stairs, spewing more faux profanity.)*

JEAN. Profanity, for us kids, was strictly verboten. But my old man? That day my father wove a tapestry of obscenity that, as far as we know, is still hanging in space over Lake Michigan. And Mother always tried to divert our attention from it.

MOTHER. Well … uh … What do you boys want for Christmas?

(#4b: "An Opening!")

JEAN. An opening!

ENSEMBLE *(as if from thin air)*.
AHHHHHHHHHHH

JEAN. I knew the old man would never get me the gun for Christmas. Maybe I'd convince Mom. I only had twenty-three days left. How could I make the case that the Red Ryder wasn't just a Christmas present—it was a necessity!?

RALPHIE *(measured, deliberate)*.
GOTTA FIND A SUBTLE WAY TO SAY IT
PLAY IT CAREFUL DON'T SEEM DESP'RATE
OR I'M DONE
GET THE RED RYDER CARBINE-ACTION BB GUN

RANDY. I want a toy zeppelin that lights up and makes noises.

MOTHER. That's nice … Ralphie?

JEAN. Now I knew the moment called for nuance and nonchalance. But sometimes you just—

RALPHIE *(blurting out quickly and excitedly)*. An Official Red Ryder carbine-action 200-shot Range Model air rifle with a compass in the stock and a–uh–uh—

JEAN *(sensing the impending doom)*. Oh, no! My tongue short-circuited my brain. I was dead. Even before she opened her mouth, I knew what was coming.

MOTHER. Ralphie—you'll shoot your eye out.

(RALPHIE slumps back into his chair.)

JEAN. Ah! It was the classic "Mother BB Gun Block." That deadly phrase uttered many times before by hundreds of mothers was not surmountable by any means known to kid-dom. I had to immediately rebuild the dike.

RALPHIE *(weakly)*. Heh, heh … I was just kidding. I guess I'd like, uh—some Tinkertoys.

JEAN *(disgusted at the very thought)*. *Tinkertoys?!* I couldn't believe my own ears. She'd never buy it …

MOTHER. All right boys, time for school.

JEAN. Who could I turn to next?

(MOTHER retrieves RANDY's snowsuit.)

MOTHER. Ralphie, put on your things. Here, Randy, let me help you.

(She begins to stuff RANDY into his snowsuit as RALPHIE goes to put on his outerwear.)

RANDY *(a prolonged whine)*. Mom, it's too cold to go to school.

JEAN *(as MOTHER continues dressing RANDY)*. Hah … There was no question of staying home. It never entered anyone's mind. It was a heartier time, and Miss Shields was a hardier teacher than the present breed. Cold in Hohman was something that was accepted, like air, clouds, parents—a fact of nature, and as such could not be used in any fraudulent scheme to stay out of school. And getting ready to go to school was like preparing for extended deep-sea diving.

(Through various and somewhat violent means, MOTHER stuffs, shakes, jiggles, crams and jams RANDY into his snowsuit. Lots of whining and complaining and squealing and grunting. Once in, his arms stick straight out from his sides. MOTHER wraps a scarf fully around RANDY's head, covering his face.)

RANDY *(completely indecipherable, speech obscured by heavy layers of clothing)*. I can't put my arms down!

MOTHER. What did you say?

RANDY *(again, indecipherable)*. I can't put my arms down!

RALPHIE. Ah, Ma, we're gonna be late.

MOTHER. Just wait, Ralphie.

RANDY *(desperately, still obscured)*. I can't put my arms down!

(MOTHER unwinds the scarf enough to expose RANDY's face.)

RANDY *(cont'd, tearfully, clearly for the first time)*. I can't put my arms down!

(MOTHER presses RANDY's arms to his sides. They pop right back up when she lets them go. Again, she firmly holds them to his sides. A beat. The arms shoot back up again.)

JEAN. Solutions are sometimes very practical in Indiana.

MOTHER *(exasperated)*. You'll put your arms down when you get to school.

(As RANDY hollers in protest, she re-wraps the scarf to cover his mouth.)

(#4c: "The Path to School")

SCENE 3

(A path leading to school. Soon afterward.

SCHWARTZ, FLICK and one other BOY enter.)

SCHWARTZ *(an ongoing debate, he argues with arrogance).* Hey listen, smartass. I asked my old man about sticking your tongue to a flagpole in the winter, and he says it'll stick to the pole, just like I told you.

FLICK *(with healthy confidence).* Ah, baloney. What would your old man know about anything?

JEAN. Schwartz and Flick, my two best friends. My fellow wimps. All for one, one for all.

SCHWARTZ. My old man knows, 'cause he once saw a guy stick his tongue to a railroad track on a bet, and the fire department had to come and get his tongue unstuck.

FLICK. You're full of beans, and so's your old man.

(ESTHER JANE and MARY BETH enter, chatting animatedly, followed by RALPHIE and RANDY.)

RALPHIE. Hey fellas, wait up!

(RANDY struggles to keep up. He falls, immobile.)

RANDY *(tries repeatedly to get up but can't).* I can't get up. *(Trying.)* I can't get up. I can't get up! *(Hysterical.)* Ralphie, I can't get up! Come on, Ralphie! Wait up! *(Whimpers.)* Come on, guys!

RALPHIE. Let's go, Randy, we're gonna be late!

RANDY. I can't! I fell down, and I can't get up!

ESTHER JANE. Go help your brother, Ralphie.

RALPHIE *(reluctantly).* Oh, all right.

(#5: "When You're a Wimp")

(RALPHIE tries to help RANDY up. An ominous chord of music is heard. SCUT FARKUS and GROVER DILL leap in with a horrifying roar.)

FARKUS & DILL. Ha, ha, ha, ha!

JEAN *(with paralyzing fear)*. Scut Farkus and Grover Dill, the bully and his toady.

DILL *(threatening, booming)*. Muah, ha, ha, ha, ha!

JEAN. We were about to be pummeled!

DILL. Come here, you wimp!

RALPHIE. Oh, no.

JEAN. These were the kind of meatheads who grow up bashing in car grills and becoming mafia hit men … or captains of industry.

FARKUS. Who's ready to say "uncle?"

ALL KIDS *(except FARKUS and DILL, charged)*.
    ON EV'RY PLAYGROUND
    THERE'S A WAR TAKING PLACE
    BETWEEN THE BULLIES
    AND THE WIMPS THAT THEY CHASE
(Resigned to their fate.)
    AND IF YOU'RE PART OF THE PACK
    THAT'S ALWAYS UNDER ATTACK,
    YOU QUICKLY LEARN THAT YOU DON'T FIGHT BACK.

(Throughout the number, the kids are tortured by the bullies. Handing over lunch money, homework, food, and receiving wedgies, noogies and the like.)

ALL KIDS *(except FARKUS and DILL, cont'd)*.
    WHEN YOU'RE A WIMP
    THEY KNOW THAT YOU DON'T HAVE THE GUTS

FLICK.
>AND YOU WAIT EVERYDAY TO GET KICKED IN THE
>NU—

(FLICK gets faux-kicked below the belt and reacts ac-cordingly.)

ALL KIDS *(except FARKUS and DILL).*
>YOU TAKE IT AGAIN AND AGAIN
>WHEN YOU'RE A WIMP!
>WHEN YOU'RE A WIMP!

(FARKUS grabs RALPHIE.)

FARKUS. OK, Ralphie, say it!

RALPHIE. Uncle!

FARKUS. I—can't—hear—you.

RALPHIE. Uncle! Uncle! UNCLE!
>YOU DO HIS HOMEWORK
>IF A QUESTION IS MISSED
>YA GET TA' ANSWER
>TO THE POUND OF HIS FIST!

ALL KIDS *(except FARKUS and DILL).*
>HE GIVES THAT THREATENING GLANCE
>AND YOU START WETTIN' YOUR PANTS
>IT'S KINDA CLEAR THAT YOU GOT NO CHANCE!
>
>WHEN YOU'RE A WIMP
>YOU DON'T EVEN TRY TO ESCAPE

SCHWARTZ *(defeated).*
>WHEN YOU ACT LIKE A FRUIT
>YOU GET CRUSHED LIKE A GRAPE

ALL KIDS *(except FARKUS and DILL).*
>YOU TRY TO SURVIVE TILL YOU'RE TEN

(FARKUS stares menacingly as kids react and scream.)

ALL KIDS *(except FARKUS and DILL, cont'd).*
   WHEN YOU'RE A WIMP!
   WHEN YOU'RE A WIMP!

(FARKUS and DILL exit, snickering, satisfied with their plunder.)

ALL KIDS *(except FARKUS and DILL, cont'd).*
   BUT OH
   THE DAY YOU GROW
   IT'LL BE SUBLIME
   AT PAYBACK TIME

(Forming their own wimp army.)

FLICK, RALPHIE & SCHWARTZ.
   YOU'LL STRETCH SIX FEET OVERNIGHT,

GIRL.
   YOU'LL PICK ONE HECK OF A FIGHT

ALL KIDS.
   AND FIN'LLY SLUG EV'RY THUG IN SIGHT!

   WHEN YOU'RE A WIMP
   YOU PATIENTLY WAIT FOR THE DAY
   WHEN THE TABLES HAVE TURNED
   AND YOU'RE MAKIN' 'EM PAY.

   IMAGINE HOW HELPLESS THEY'LL SEEM
   WHEN YOU'RE TWISTING THEIR ARMS TILL THEY
      SCREAM.
   YEAH, YOU GOTTA HOLD ON TO THAT DREAM
   WHEN YOU'RE A WIMP!
   WHEN YOU'RE A WIMP!
   WHEN YOU'RE A

KIDS 1.
   WIMP!

KIDS 2.
    WIMP!

KIDS 3.
    WIMP!

(As the KIDS celebrate and start to exit toward school, FARKUS and DILL return to scare them off.)

(#5a: "After Wimp")

(DILL throws FARKUS a congratulatory punch on the arm. FARKUS reciprocates. DILL, proving his might, punches FARKUS, a bit harder this time. FARKUS responds even harder, reminding DILL who's boss.)

JEAN. Although I had survived the wrath of the feared, arm-twisting twosome, there was no avoiding the fact that the coveted air rifle was in serious jeopardy. I couldn't even convince my own mother I needed it! I had to find another way.

(School bell rings.)

SCENE 4

(The classroom. A few minutes later.)

MISS SHIELDS *(prim, stuffy)*. Good morning, class.

KIDS *(in muffled, unenthused voices)*. Good morning, Miss Shields.

MISS SHIELDS. Children. Our first activity of the day will be an in-class theme—

(The KIDS groan.)

MISS SHIELDS *(cont'd)*. Entitled: "What I Want for Christmas."

(The KIDS perk up, excited. Especially RALPHIE.)

(#5b: "What I Want for Christmas")

JEAN *(pleased with his luck).* I had found another way!

MISS SHIELDS. And, as always, I expect good penmanship, careful conjugation, proper punctuation and close attention to the margins. *Margins … (Frustration boils over, directed at RALPHIE.)* MARGINS! You may begin.

(MISS SHIELDS discretely takes a book from her desk and begins to read. The KIDS pull out their notebooks and pencils and begin to write.)

JEAN. If I could get Miss Shields to sympathize with my plight, she might phone my mother and implore her to get me that gun. That piece of cold blue steel would soon be mine. If I could just stay inside the margins. Rarely had the words poured from my penny pencil with such feverish fluidity. I remember to this day the glorious wingéd phrases and concise imagery of that theme.

RALPHIE *(to himself as he writes).* "What I want for Christmas is a Red Ryder BB gun with a compass in the stock and this thing that tells time." *(Impressed with himself.)* Wow, that's great! "I don't think a football is a very good Christmas present. But, I think that everybody should have a Red Ryder BB gun. You never know when you'll need it."

VILLAIN *(menacingly, appearing suddenly from out of nowhere).* Ha ha ha!

(#6: "Ralphie to the Rescue!")

(As RALPHIE's fantasy begins, we see a VILLAIN grab MISS SHIELDS and tie her to the desk. He's going to blow her up with TNT. The KIDS scream and take cover.)

KIDS. AAAHHH!!!

MISS SHIELDS.
AAAHHH!!!

RALPHIE *(on high alert, dramatic).*
YOUR TEACHER
IN TROUBLE
SO GET THERE ON THE DOUBLE
OR SHE'LL FACE HER DOOM

MISS SHIELDS *(a desperate yelp).* Raaaalphie!! Do something!!

RALPHIE.
THE TENSION
IS MOUNTING
ONE MINUTE LEFT AND COUNTING
TILL SHE GOES *KABOOM!*

(The VILLAIN laughs.)

MISS SHIELDS *(high drama).*
WON'T YOU SAVE ME, RALPHIE?
TELL THE SCOUNDREL TO SURRENDER?

RALPHIE *(valiant).*
I'LL SAVE THE DAY!

MISS SHIELDS.
OH, HE'S GOT ME, RALPHIE!
I COULD DIE IN THIS DISASTER
FASTER!

RALPHIE.
HOLD ON, I'M ON MY WAY!

(With the help of JEAN and the KIDS, RALPHIE becomes a fantasy cowboy. A self-assured, gutsy and gallant hero. Cowboy hat, boots, chaps, BB gun and all.)

RALPHIE *(cont'd)*.
> RALPHIE TO THE RESCUE
> OH!
> RALPHIE TO THE RESCUE
> OH!
>
> ONE THING TO DO
> TIME TO TURN TO OLD BLUE
> NOW LET HER GO!

(RALPHIE shoots the match out of the VILLAIN's hand. The VILLAIN screams and runs away.)

RALPHIE *(cont'd)*.
> YIPPEE-KAY-O

MISS SHIELDS *(thanking him)*. My hero!

(BANKROBBERS, the Spaghetti Western sort, TELLERS [SCHWARTZ and BOY] and a bank appear.)

TELLERS. AAAAHH!

RALPHIE.
> WE'RE STUCK IN A STICKUP

BANKROBBER 1.
> *WE'VE GOT SOME CASH TO PICK UP!*

BANKROBBER 2 *(demanding)*.
> FILL THE BAG WITH LOOT!

KIDS. AHHHHH!

RALPHIE.
> THEY'RE TELLIN' THE TELLER

BANKROBBER 1.
> NOW HAND IT OVER, FELLER

BANKROBBER 2.
>OR WE'LL HAVE TO SHOOT!

Hands in the air!

BANKROBBER 1. That's right!

(The ENSEMBLE and KIDS enter, all bank customers caught in the stickup.)

KIDS.
>WON'T YOU HELP US, RALPHIE?
>TELL THESE ROBBERS TO RELEASE US

TELLER 1 *(SCHWARTZ, operatic and highly dramatic).*
>DON'T LET ME DIE!

BANKROBBERS.
>TRY AND STOP US, RALPHIE!

RALPHIE.
>HOPE YOU'RE READY FOR SOME PAYBACK

TELLER 1 *(SCHWARTZ, to the KIDS).*
>*STAY BACK!*

RALPHIE *(cocksure, confident).*
>FORGET THE FBI

TOWNSMEN 1, 2 & 3.
>FORGET THE FBI!

RALPHIE.	TOWNSWOMEN.	TOWNSMEN.
RALPHIE TO THE RESCUE	OH	
OH!	OH	OH
RALPHIE & KIDS.		
RALPHIE TO THE RESCUE	OH	
OH!		OH

KIDS *(except RALPHIE).*
>HE'S HERE TO BOOK
EV'RY BANK-ROBBIN' CROOK

ALL.
>SO DROP THE DOUGH!

(RALPHIE shoots the stolen money bags and guns out of the BANKROBBERS' hands. They run off in terror.)

ALL *(cont'd).*
>YIPPEE KAY-O!

PRAIRIE ENSEMBLE.
>GET 'EM, COWBOY!
COWBOY RALPHIE!

(Á la hillbillies.)

>THE FAV'RITE SON OF INDIANA
WITH HIS GUN AND HIS BANDANNA

PRAIRIE MEN.
>RIDIN' HIGH!

PRAIRIE WOMEN.
>HIGH!

PRAIRIE ENSEMBLE.
>GET 'EM, COWBOY!
COWBOY RALPHIE!

PRAIRIE WOMEN.
>JUST IN TIME TO FIGHT SOME CRIME
JUST LIKE RED, HE'LL SHOOT 'EM DEAD

PRAIRIE ENSEMBLE.
>YIPPEE KAY, YIPPEE KAY
YIPPEE KAY, YIPPEE KAY
YIPPEE KAY, YIPPEE KAY-O!

(Dance section: RALPHIE appears with his Tonto-esque sidekick, played by RANDY, who is dressed in Native American garb. RALPHIE pounds a tribal drum and RANDY does a war whoop.

RALPHIE exits. RANDY smokes a peace pipe. His solitude is disrupted by an ESCAPED PRISONER, still in prison stripes and intent on kidnapping him.)

RANDY.
  HELP ME, RALPHIE!

(RALPHIE re-enters with his Red Ryder BB gun, primed to save the day.)

RALPHIE.
  RALPHIE TO THE RESCUE
  RALPHIE TO THE RESCUE

(RALPHIE shoots the pants off the ESCAPED PRISONER, revealing his silky boxer shorts. The ESCAPED PRISONER runs off, terrified. RANDY shares his peace pipe with RALPHIE, who chokes from his first inhale. They ride off in the sunset together as other tap-dancing KIDS ride in on stick horses. One BOY's horse is stolen by another.)

BOY *(in anguish)*. I want my horsey back! Someone help me get my horsey back!

(RALPHIE rides on to, once again, save the day. After a struggle with the perpetrator, he retrieves the BOY's horse and returns it to its rightful owner.)

BOY. Thanks, partner!

(An old-fashioned saloon materializes. We see a BARTENDER, CUSTOMERS and CAN-CAN GIRLS. A BANDIT [played by DILL] drunkenly enters the saloon, orders

a drink and seizes CAN-CAN GIRLFRIEND. RALPHIE enters to save her. After a showdown with the BANDIT, he uses some BB gun shots to make him dance and flee the scene. Out of danger, RALPHIE and CAN-CAN GIRL-FRIEND run into each other's arms in slow motion.

As the lovers celebrate, BLACK BART [played by FARKUS] and the BANDIT enter with MOTHER, THE OLD MAN and RANDY in tow. They have kidnapped and hogtied the PARKERS.)

ENSEMBLE *(terrified, shaking in their boots).* Black Bart!

(An old fashioned bar brawl ensues. Fists and bottles flying. This is perhaps played out in slow motion as well. There is a struggle for possession of the PARKERS—BLACK BART and the BANDIT threaten RALPHIE with their hand pistols when suddenly RALPHIE pulls out his Red Ryder rifle. He clearly has the upper hand.)

BLACK BART & BANDIT *(terror-stricken as they run away).* AAAAHH!!!

TOWNSMEN & TOWNSWOMEN.
    RALPHIE TO THE RESCUE

RALPHIE *(with jubilation).*
    OH!

RALPHIE & ENSEMBLE.
    RALPHIE TO THE RESCUE
    OH!

RANDY, MOTHER, THE OLD MAN & MISS SHIELDS *(proudly).*
    SO BRAVE AND SO BOLD
    AND HE'S JUST NINE YEARS OLD

RALPHIE.
> WHEN I'VE GOT OLD BLUE, I'M A BORN BUCKAROO

ENSEMBLE.
> A BOY AND HIS GUN RIDING OFF IN THE SUN
> JUST WATCH HIM
> GO! GO! GO!

RALPHIE *(triumphant).*
> YIPPEE KAY-O!

(When the song ends, we are once again in the classroom with the KIDS in their seats, RALPHIE still lost in his cowboy fantasy. MISS SHIELDS is engrossed in her romance novel.)

MISS SHIELDS *(rapturously).* And then he kissed her gently on the … *(She quickly snaps out of her fantasy and slams her book shut.)* All right, time to hand in your papers. *(Begins to collect the themes. To RALPHIE as he daydreams.)* Yoo-hoo, Ralphie. Ralphie?

RALPHIE. Huh? *(Quickly back to earth.)* Ah! Oh … almost finished.

(#6a: "After Ralphie to the Rescue!")

RALPHIE *(cont'd, sotto voce as he writes).* "I think everyone should have a Red Ryder BB gun. And I think a Red Ryder BB gun would be a very good Christmas present."

(He hands MISS SHIELDS the theme, feeling very satisfied with himself. He is isolated in a spotlight as the scene shifts to the Parker family house. During JEAN's speech, RALPHIE's mood changes from hopeful to distraught.)

JEAN. I raced home imagining Miss Shields reading my theme that very night. Swooning, overwhelmed by a work of rhetorical genius. An A-plus at the very least. But there was just one problem. A whole week went by, and she still hadn't graded the themes. Gradually, expectation turned to anxiety, then deep despair.

RALPHIE *(desperation is growing as time is slipping away)*. I'VE GOT ONE SHOT AND IT'S SEVENTEEN DAYS AWAY …

SCENE 5

(The Parker family house. A week later.

Lights come up on the kitchen. MOTHER is busy preparing dinner.)

MOTHER *(calling to upstairs)*. Ralphie … Randy! Time for supper. I just heard your father pull up. He'll be famished. Hurry up now and wash up.

(RALPHIE and RANDY enter from upstairs.

The BUMPUS HOUNDS are heard barking from offstage. THE OLD MAN enters, grabs the mail and hurries to escape the dogs.)

THE OLD MAN *(growling)*. Get out of here you rotten mala-futin' mangy mutts! *(He enters the house, yelling through the window.)* Confloggers, muttjoggers! You'll pay for this, Bumpus! *(The BUMPUS HOUNDS appear in the window.)* You and your hog-huggin', mange-moltin' hounds! Get out of here! Go on, get out of here! *(The dogs retreat.)*

MOTHER *(sweetly)*. Hello, dear. Did you have a good day?

THE OLD MAN *(tired, frustrated)*. I did till quitting time. Then the Olds wouldn't start. Again. So, I had to get a jump. Needs a new battery. Those things are up to six dollars apiece these days.

MOTHER. Well, dear, a big plate of meatloaf and cabbage should cheer you up.

THE OLD MAN *(under his breath)*. Oh, sure.

MOTHER. Now everyone go and wash up. Dinner's getting cold.

RANDY *(yelping)*. No, I don't need to. I washed my hands yesterday.

(THE OLD MAN picks up the protesting RANDY, and they exit upstairs, followed by RALPHIE.)

(#7: "What a Mother Does")

MOTHER *(constantly moving, cleaning, organizing, slicing, scooping and serving food, clearing dishes, deriving great joy from her role as a mother)*.
NEW STAINS ON THE RUG
STRAY SOCKS ON THE STAIR
AND PILES OF PAPER APPEARING
RIGHT OUT OF THIN AIR.

BUT THE SHEETS HAVE BEEN WASHED
THE PANTS HAVE BEEN PRESSED
THE FLOORS HAVE BEEN SCRUBBED
LIKE A WOMAN POSSESSED

AND WE'RE STEADY AND STABLE
A MEAL ON THE TABLE
EACH EVENING BECAUSE
THAT'S WHAT A MOTHER DOES

(THE OLD MAN, RALPHIE and RANDY enter. All sit except for RANDY, who is under the table.)

MOTHER *(cont'd)*. Randy, sit down and let's eat.

RANDY *(slumps into his chair and stares at his food)*. Awwwww …

JEAN. Every family has a kid who won't eat. In our case, it was my brother.

RALPHIE. Can I have some more meatloaf?

(MOTHER goes and gets the meatloaf.)

JEAN. My kid brother had not eaten voluntarily in over three years.

(MOTHER brings the meatloaf to RALPHIE. She sits down to begin eating.)

THE OLD MAN *(unaware that she has just sat down).* More potatoes, dear.

(MOTHER gets back up and goes to get the potatoes.)

JEAN. My mother hadn't eaten a hot meal for herself in fifteen years.

MOTHER.
> SIT DOWN TO STAND UP
> YOU'RE BACK ON YOUR FEET
> SERVE SECONDS AND THIRDS
> WHILE YOU'VE STILL GOT A BOY WHO WON'T EAT

RANDY *(pushing his food around his plate, repulsed).* Aw, jeez.

MOTHER.
> BUT A MOM HAS HER WAYS
> A MOM KNOWS HER KID
> SHE'LL GET HIM TO EAT
> WITHOUT KNOWING HE DID
>
> IT'S JUST ONE OF HER TALENTS
> SHE KEEPS LIFE IN BALANCE
> AMID ALL THE BUZZ
> THAT'S WHAT A MOTHER DOES.

MOTHER *(cont'd, attempting to use guilt to make him eat).* Starving people would be glad to have that.

RANDY. Awww … Meatloaf, smeatloaf, double beetloaf. I hate meatloaf.

THE OLD MAN. Where's the screwdriver and the plumber's helper? I'll pry his mouth open and stuff it in.

JEAN. And he would have. But my mother was a bit more subtle.

MOTHER *(as if playing a game)*. Randy? How do little piggies go?

(RANDY snorts like a pig and continues to do so intermittently.)

MOTHER *(cont'd, encouraging him)*. That's right! Oink, oink. Nice little piggies.

JEAN. My brother was deep into *The Three Little Pigs*.

MOTHER. Now, how do little piggies eat? There's your trough. How do little piggies eat? Be a good boy. Show Mommy how the piggies eat.

(Suddenly, RANDY bends forward, shoves his face into the plate and begins to gobble food frantically, giggling all the while as MOTHER coaxes him on.)

RALPHIE *(under his breath)*. Gosh.

THE OLD MAN *(under his breath)*. Jesus. *(Or "jeez.")*

JEAN. It *was* disgusting.

MOTHER. Mommy's little piggy. That's right. *(She moves on to her next set of tasks.)*
> ONE THING DOWN, A MILLION MORE YOU'VE MISSED
> THE PLATES, THE PANS, KEEP CROSSING OFF THE LIST
> HOMEWORK, PJS, GET THE KIDS TO BED
> CHOOSE A CHRISTMAS STORY TO BE READ
>
> YES, CHRISTMAS IS HERE
> THERE'S SO MUCH TO DO
> A HOUSE TO LOOK FESTIVE
> A FAM'LY THAT'S COUNTING ON YOU

WITH TINSEL TO BUY AND STOCKINGS TO STUFF
TO MAKE THEM FORGET THAT THE TIMES HAVE
    BEEN TOUGH.
YOU'RE A MOM ON A MISSION TO KEEP UP TRADITION
COOKIES AND CAROLS AND LAUGHTER IN BARRELS
TILL YOU HEAR THEM SAY

"YOU'VE MADE CHRISTMAS DAY
THE VERY BEST CHRISTMAS THAT THERE EVER WAS"

'CAUSE THAT'S WHAT A MOTHER
WHAT ANY GOOD MOTHER
THAT'S WHAT A MOTHER DOES.

THE OLD MAN *(flipping through a pile of mail on the table)*. Bills … bills … bills … These bills are never ending.

JEAN *(referring to the envelope THE OLD MAN is about to open)*. Ah, another brilliant idea …

THE OLD MAN. Hmm. Here's a letter with no stamp on it. It's addressed to you.

MOTHER. Me?

THE OLD MAN. How can they deliver a letter with no stamp on it?

MOTHER *(opens the letter, dismissive)*. Oh, it's a silly ad for a kid's BB gun. Those things are dangerous!

(#7a: "Miss Shields Fantasy")

(She throws it into the trash. Music: sting. RALPHIE drops his head in defeat.)

JEAN. *Rats*! My fevered brain seethed with the effort to come up with an infinitely subtle device to implant the air rifle indelibly into my parents' consciousness without their being aware of it.

(A beat.)

RALPHIE *(abruptly, concocting a story)*. Flick says he saw some grizzly bears near Pulaski's candy store the other day.

JEAN. My parents looked at me as if I had lobsters coming out of my ears.

MOTHER. That's—quite interesting, dear.

JEAN *(frustrated)*. If I couldn't get my parents' attention, it would have to be up to Miss Shields. She *had* to get those papers graded soon.

(Another fantasy as MISS SHIELDS enters the Parker family house in a puff of smoke, lavishing RALPHIE with exaggerated praise.)

MISS SHIELDS. Mr. and Mrs. Parker, your extraordinary son Ralph has written the theme I've been waiting for all my life. "What I want for Christmas is a Red Ryder BB gun with a compass in the stock and this *thing* that tells time!" Sheer poetry. And the penmanship, the conjugation, the punctuation. *(She salivates over this.)* All contained in the tightly constrained dictates of the margins. I can hardly *control* myself. Anyway, Ralph has convinced me beyond a doubt, through his magnificent and eloquent theme, that it is absolutely necessary that he be given a Red Ryder BB gun for the protection of your family. After all, grizzly bears were spotted near Pulaski's candy store the other day. *(She winks at RALPHIE.)* Thank you, Mr. and Mrs. Parker, for your time. And for Ralph—my prize, A-plus, plus, plus, plus, plus, plus student!

(She exits as quickly as she appeared, and the fantasy is over though RALPHIE remains entranced.)

MOTHER *(to RALPHIE, monotone)*. Eat your cabbage, Ralphie. You need your roughage.

(Back to reality, RALPHIE heaves a sigh of despair.

The front doorbell rings.)

THE OLD MAN. Well, who's that?

MOTHER. I'm not sure …

THE OLD MAN. It's almost seven!

(MOTHER goes to answer it. JEAN enters, wearing a telegram delivery hat.)

JEAN *(as MAILMAN)*. Telegram for you folks, Mrs. Parker.

(He hands the telegram to MOTHER and exits.)

THE OLD MAN. What is it?

MOTHER. A telegram.

THE OLD MAN *(nervously)*. What's it say?

MOTHER *(handing him the telegram)*. It's addressed to you.

(THE OLD MAN slowly opens the telegram.)

MOTHER *(cont'd)*. Well … ?

THE OLD MAN *(trembling, after a moment)*. Look. Read it.

MOTHER *(at first, fearing the worst)*. "Dear Mr. Parker. Congratulations! You have won a major award in our $50,000 'Great Figures of World Literature Contest.' It will arrive by special messenger tonight. Congratulations! You arc a winner!"

THE OLD MAN *(dances around the kitchen, exuberant)*. I. Am. A. Winner. I'm a winner! I'm a winner!!!

MOTHER. But a winner of what?

THE OLD MAN. It could be anything. A new car, a trip to Paris. A guy in Terre Haute won a bowling alley.

MOTHER *(practical, skeptical)*. How could they deliver a bowling alley?

THE OLD MAN *(stumped for a moment)*. Well … they could deliver a deed, for cripessake.

(The doorbell rings again. The PARKERS freeze.)

THE OLD MAN *(cont'd, with a hushed reverence).* It's here! Omigod, it's here!

(JEAN, now dressed as a delivery man, and two more DELIVERY MEN have entered and made their way to the front door, carrying a large crate. THE OLD MAN answers the door.)

JEAN. Frank Parker?
THE OLD MAN. Yeah?
JEAN. Sign here.

(JEAN hands a clipboard and a pen to THE OLD MAN, who scribbles frantically. JEAN calls to the DELIVERY MEN.)

JEAN *(cont'd).* OK, haul it in.

(7b: "Haul It In")

(The DELIVERY MEN enter and deposit the crate in the living room.)

THE OLD MAN *(cont'd, eagerly).* Well, what is it?

(JEAN shrugs. A very long pause as THE PARKERS stare at the giant crate.)

THE OLD MAN *(cont'd).* What is it?
JEAN *(annoyed).* I don't know.

(JEAN and the DELIVERY MEN exit as THE OLD MAN begins to roughly examine the crate, recklessly lowering it long-ways on the floor.)

MOTHER. Careful, dear. Look what it says on the side.

(THE OLD MAN looks to see the word "fragile.")

THE OLD MAN *(sounding it out, exclaiming with ecstasy).* *Fra-gee-lay.* It must be Italian. I won an Italian prize. *(In a thick Italian accent.)* Fra-gee-lay!

MOTHER *(gently).* I think that says fragile, honey.

THE OLD MAN. Oh, yeah.

(#8: "A Major Award")

THE OLD MAN *(cont'd).* Crowbar. Get me a crowbar. And a hammer. Get me a hammer.

(RALPHIE and RANDY quickly exit as THE OLD MAN jumps atop the crate, overjoyed.)

THE OLD MAN *(cont'd.)*
 HERE'S THE PROOF I'M SOMEONE
 I'M A SOMEONE, VERY WISE
 WHEN YOU'RE THIS ASTUTE
 YOU GET SALUTED WITH A PRIZE

 AND WHEN THAT PRIZE ARRIVES IN A GIANT
  WOODEN CRATE
 YOU KNOW IT'S SOMETHIN' GREAT!
 HA!

(RALPHIE and RANDY rush in with the crowbar and hammer respectively. THE OLD MAN begins to work at opening the crate, swiftly and excitedly.)

JEAN. The old man worked in supercharged haste to lay bare his hard won symbol of victory.

THE OLD MAN *(removes the lid).*
 OH, MR. PARKER
 WHO COULD BELIEVE THE
 GLORY OF THE GIFT
 THAT YOU'RE ABOUT TO RECEIVE?

(THE OLD MAN reaches inside the crate and holds up a large plastic leg in a seductive fishnet stocking and a black high-heeled shoe.)

MOTHER *(aghast)*. What is it?

THE OLD MAN. A—leg.

MOTHER *(after a pause)*. But—what is it?

THE OLD MAN *(a bit edgy, defensive)*. Well, it's a leg. Like a statuc.

MOTHER. A statue?

RANDY. Whoopee, a statue!

RALPHIE *(feeling the leg, seduced)* We won a statue …

(MOTHER quickly takes RALPHIE's hand off of the leg.)

THE OLD MAN. Wait a minute. There's something else in the box.

MOTHER. What?

(THE OLD MAN bends down and fishes inside the crate. He can't believe his good fortune.)

THE OLD MAN. Holy smokes! Do you know what this is?

RALPHIE & RANDY. What?

(THE OLD MAN reveals the leg, now assembled with a shade.)

THE OLD MAN *(delighted)*. It's a lamp!

MOTHER *(confused)*. It's a lamp?

THE OLD MAN *(with growing admiration)*. It's … It's …
IT'S A MAJOR AWARD!
I WON A MAJOR AWARD!

I WON A GRAND SLAM, BIG FAT
WAM-BAM, "TAKE THAT!" AWARD

I WON A MAJOR AWARD
I WON A MAJOR AWARD
WHO WON? I WON!
IT'S ME? I SEE!
WELL, GEE!
IT'S A MAJOR AWARD!

Wow, this is exactly what we need for the front window.

MOTHER. Now, dear. I'm not sure the front window is the best—

JEAN. The snap of a few sparks, a quick whiff of ozone and the lamp blazed forth in unparalleled glory.

(THE OLD MAN plugs the lamp in. It sizzles and pops, giving THE OLD MAN a momentary electrical shock. Then it lights up. THE OLD MAN gasps in reverence. RALPHIE and RANDY cheer.)

THE OLD MAN *(in deep awe)*. Ain't that something!

MOTHER *(under her breath)*. It's … something, all right.

THE OLD MAN. Hey, wait! I want to see it from outside.

(The scene shifts to an exterior view of the lamp in the window with THE OLD MAN now on Cleveland Street and the rest of THE PARKERS inside. He motions to MOTHER, directing the placement of the lamp.)

JEAN. The lamp, to my mother's consternation, could be seen up and down Cleveland Street.

THE OLD MAN. You should see it from out here!

MOTHER *(mumbles)*. Oh, I can see it fine from here.

THE OLD MAN. Honey, move it a little forward!

MOTHER *(reluctantly)*. Forward?

THE OLD MAN. Yeah, toward me!

(Three TOWNSMEN enter. They jeer him.)

TOWNSMAN 1.
WHAT ON EARTH IS THAT?

THE OLD MAN.
IS WHAT?

TOWNSMAN 1.
THAT WINDOW, SUCH A GLOW!

THE OLD MAN.
OH!
IT'S A BIG-TIME HONOR, AN AWARD

TOWNSMAN 2.
I'D NEVER KNOW!

THE OLD MAN.
NOW, THIS IS PATENT PROOF
THAT'CHUR NEIGHBOR IS A CHAMP

TOWNSMAN 3.
IT LOOKS JUST LIKE A LAMP

(More TOWNSMEN and TOWNSWOMEN are entering.)

THE OLD MAN *(defensively)*.
THAT THERE'S A STATUE
A FINE WORK OF ART
A PRIZE THAT THEY BESTOW
UPON THE EXTRA SUPER SMART

(He tries to convince the TOWNSWOMEN of his victory.)

FRIENDS, IT'S A MAJOR AWARD
I WON A MAJOR AWARD!

TOWNSMAN 4.
WHO WON?

TOWNSMAN 5.
HE WON?

TOWNSMEN 1, 2 & 3.
IT'S HE!

TOWNSMEN 4 & 5.
I SEE!

THE OLD MAN
WELL, GEE ...

TOWNSMEN *(now seeing the light).*
HE WON A MAJOR AWARD!

IT'S A TROPHY HE CAN CHERISH
WHAT A BEAUTY

TOWNSWOMEN.
OH, IT'S GARISH

TOWNSMEN 1.
HE'S A WINNER

TOWNSMEN 2.
THAT'S FOR CERTAIN

MOTHER *(from inside the house, meekly).*
MAYBE WE COULD CLOSE THE CURTAIN

TOWNSWOMEN.
FOR A WINDOW, SLIGHTLY OVERBOARD ...

THE OLD MAN.
DON'T YOU GET IT? LADIES, IT'S A MAJOR AWARD!

TOWNSWOMEN *(in sudden and heightened realization).*
A MAJOR AWARD?

THE OLD MAN.
A MAJOR AWARD

TOWNSWOMEN.
A MAJOR AWARD?

TOWNSMEN.
A MAJOR AWARD

TOWNSPEOPLE *(with adulation).*
FRANK PARKER DID IT
HOW REMARKABLY GRAND!
FRANK PARKER DID IT
NOW THE WORLD WILL UNDERSTAND

(The ENSEMBLE exits as we focus on THE OLD MAN, in spotlight. In fantasy, he delivers an acceptance speech for his major award.)

THE OLD MAN *(overwhelmingly self-indulgent).*
I'M THE GENIUS ON CLEVELAND STREET

No one ever believed in me. The kids used to call me "Franky Franky, dumb and lanky. Can't play ball or use a hanky." Until fifth grade on my report card, near the bottom under "comments," my teacher Mrs. Millsap wrote, *(With pride and nostalgia, he struggles through the quote.)* "Frank Parker shows some potential." *(Almost in tears.)*

A TASTE OF VICTORY, SO SWEET

I'd like to acknowledge all the other contestants who were eligible for this most hallowed honor. Gentlemen—you were all terrific. I guess I just had a leg up on the competition! *(Cackling at his own wit.)* Hey—if I'm lucky, next year I'll win the rest of her! *(Again, beside himself with self-satisfaction.)*

NOW WATCH IT IGNITE
THIS LITTLE LIGHT OF MINE
LET IT SHINE!

(Through dance, THE OLD MAN's leg lamp fantasies come true in Hollywood fashion. TOWNSPEOPLE re-enter as sparkling showgirls and showmen with leg lamps lit. At one point, MOTHER appears in a sexy leg lamp getup. THE OLD MAN delights in his Busby Berkeley leg lamp dream sequence, which culminates in a leg lamp kickline.)

THE OLD MAN & TOWNSPEOPLE.
> THE GENIUS ON CLEVELAND STREET
> HOW CAN ANY MAN COMPETE?

(The KIDS enter, each with his or her own miniature leg lamp. The stage is full of them.)

THE OLD MAN *(with building euphoria).*
> WITH A DOWNSTAGE, BIG BRASS
> FRONT PAGE, FIRST CLASS
> CLEAR CUT, RED HOT
> "LOOK WHAT I GOT"
> AWARD?

TOWNSPEOPLE.
> HE WON A MAJOR AWARD!
> HE WON A MAJOR AWARD

TOWNSPEOPLE & KIDS.
> YES, IT'S A
> TRUE SCHOLASTIC

THE OLD MAN.
> CAREFUL, IT'S PLASTIC!

TOWNSPEOPLE & KIDS.
> AWARD!
>
> WHO'D HAVE GUESSED HE GOT
> EV'RY ANSWER CORRECT?

THE OLD MAN. I did it!

TOWNSPEOPLE & KIDS.
 SO IMPRESSED HE'S A
 MAN YOU GOTTA RESPECT

ALL.
 SO COME AND MEET
 THE GENIUS ON
 CLEVELAND STREET

THE OLD MAN.
 I WON A MAJOR AWARD!

TOWNSPEOPLE.
 HE WON A MAJOR AWARD!

THE OLD MAN.
 I WON A MAJOR AWARD!

TOWNSPEOPLE.
 A MAJOR AWARD!

THE OLD MAN.
 I WON A MAJOR AWARD!

ALL.
 A MAJOR AWARD!

(#8a: "After Major Award")

SCENE 6

(The Parker family house. Early evening on December 13, 1940.

The leg lamp is lit up in the front window. MOTHER is staring worriedly at the lamp.)

JEAN. Needless to say, the leg lamp was the number one topic of conversation in the neighborhood. Despite my mother's futile protestations of the glowing electric sex display, the old man was resolute in keeping his symbol of newfound self-esteem in the front window for all to see.

(Sounds of the BUMPUS HOUNDS barking are heard.)

THE OLD MAN *(from outside)*. Shut up, you gardingle dogs. Come on, everybody! If we don't hurry, all the good trees will be gone!

MOTHER. We're coming. We're coming. Goodness gracious. Uh, I'll just be a second dear.

(She inconspicuously turns off the leg lamp during the following dialogue. RALPHIE and RANDY enter, coming down the stairs, in the middle of an argument.)

RALPHIE. I get to pick the tree out this time.

RANDY. No, I get to pick out the tree this time.

(THE OLD MAN, wearing gloves and an overcoat and carrying a tree saw, enters the living room.)

RALPHIE. You picked it out last time.

RANDY. Did not.

RALPHIE. Did too.

RANDY. Did not.

RALPHIE. Did too.

RANDY. Did not.

RALPHIE. Did too.

(This may repeat upwards of twenty times as THE OLD MAN look on incredulously.)

THE OLD MAN. Shut up! We will all pick out the tree together. And if it's one I like, we'll get it. In the car, in the car!

(MOTHER, RALPHIE and RANDY start to exit through the front door to the car. THE OLD MAN glances back and sees the leg lamp unlit.)

THE OLD MAN *(cont'd)*. Hey, who turned off the lamp? *(Moves toward the lamp.)*

MOTHER *(trying to distract him)*. We don't want to miss out on all the good trees, do we, dear?

RANDY *(impatiently)*. Yeah, come on, Dad. Let's go.

MOTHER *(an appeal)*. We don't want to waste electricity, do we, dear?

(THE OLD MAN grumbles.)

RALPHIE. Come on, Dad!

(THE OLD MAN grumbles again, then gives up and exits through the front door with THE PARKERS in tow. They get into the car.)

SCENE 7

(On the road, immediately following.)

(#9: "Parker Family Sing-along")

(THE PARKERS are singing in their car, playful and care-free. Trees swirl by.)

THE PARKERS.
WE'LL BRAVE THE BITTER WEATHER
'CAUSE IT ALL COMES DOWN TO CHRISTMAS
AND MAKE IT THROUGH TOGETHER
'CAUSE IT ALL COMES DOWN TO CHRISTMAS
WE'VE GOT ONE SHOT AND IT'S ONLY TWELVE DAYS

MOTHER.	RALPHIE & RANDY.	THE OLD MAN.
AWAY.	AWAY	
	AWAY	AWAY

THE PARKERS.
> WE HAFTA HURRY UP
> 'CAUSE IT ALL COMES DOWN TO CHRISTMAS—

(A sound of a punctured tire. The car sags and screeches to a halt.)

THE OLD MAN. Oh, flibberdygibbit! Muckerucker! Corn doodle doo.

MOTHER. What is it, dear?

THE OLD MAN. Nobody move! We have—a flat!

JEAN. My old man's tires were actually only tires in the academic sense. They were round and made of rubber. But there was so little tread, you could read the want ads of the *Tribune* right through them.

THE OLD MAN *(slightly perturbed, yet confident)*. Left front this time. I'll get the jack and change it. Four minutes. Time me.

(#9a: "Flat Tire")

THE OLD MAN *(cont'd)*. Carn fenuckle!

(He exits the car, opens the trunk and pulls out the spare tire, jack and tire iron.)

JEAN. Actually, my old man loved it. He always saw himself in the pits at the Indianapolis 500 Motor Speedway.

THE OLD MAN. All of you—stay in the car. Don't want it falling on anybody in case the jack fails. Four minutes. Go! *(Begins to change the tire.)*

MOTHER. Ralphie, go help your father change the tire.

RALPHIE *(surprised, excited)*. Really? Can I?

MOTHER. Yes.

JEAN. It was the first time it had been suggested that I help my father with anything.

(RALPHIE approaches THE OLD MAN who is fast at work.)

THE OLD MAN *(noticing RALPHIE, slightly annoyed)*. What are you doing?

RALPHIE. Mom said I should help.

THE OLD MAN *(grumbling)*. Oh, yeah? Well, get over here and hold this hubcap.

(He gives the hubcap to RALPHIE.)

THE OLD MAN *(cont'd, sternly and forcefully)*. No, not like that. Hold it like a man. Now I'm gonna put the lug nuts in it. So, for cripessake, don't move.

(Sounds of the mimed lug nuts, five in all, are heard hitting the metal hubcap as JEAN speaks.)

JEAN. So, the old man kept at it, and I held the hubcap in a death grip. When my father said, "Don't move," what he really meant was, "Don't breathe." But I was up to it. I could do it! I would do anything to prove myself worthy.

THE OLD MAN. Consarn it, krick in my knee!

(After removing the tire, THE OLD MAN lurches to a standing position, knocking the hubcap from RALPHIE's hand.)

RALPHIE *(in very slow motion, a prolonged cry)*. AAAHHH!!!

(They freeze, except for their heads, which follow the high arc of the hubcap in slow motion and then offstage to the landing of the mimed lug nuts.)

JEAN *(with exaggerated horror).* The lug nuts went flying through the air, silhouetted against the moonlit night sky. Then they were gone. Suddenly, I lost all sense of where I was or who I was with.

(9b: "F*@#!")

RALPHIE *(still very slow motion, perhaps an echo effect).* Ooooh, fffffuuuuuuuuuuuuuddddggggggeeee!

(Beat.)

JEAN *(slowly confessing).* Only I didn't say "fudge." I said the word. The big one, the queen mother of dirty words— the f-dash-dash-dash word. I had broken the verboten rule. I was awfully young to die.

THE OLD MAN *(almost bewildered).* What did you say?

RALPHIE *(petrified).* Uh—uh …

THE OLD MAN *(gritting his teeth).* That's what I thought you said. Get in the car. Go on!

(RALPHIE gets into the car as THE OLD MAN, grumbling more faux-swears, quickly mimes rounding up the lug nuts and finishes changing the tire. This time at lightning speed as he seethes with anger.)

THE OLD MAN *(under his breath).* Get the Oldsmobile, Frank. Get the Oldsmobile. Yeah, from your dead-beat brother. *(He gets into the car.)*

MOTHER *(revealing his time).* Eight minutes.

THE OLD MAN. Do you know what your son just said?

MOTHER *(innocently).* No, what?

THE OLD MAN. Oh, I'll tell you what he said. *(Swatting RANDY away.)* Randy!

(He whispers into MOTHER's ear. She gasps audibly.)

MOTHER. I can't breathe … I can't breathe!

JEAN *(full of doom).* It was all over. I was dead. What would it be—the guillotine, a hanging, the chair, the rack, Chinese water torture? No. Mere child's play compared with what awaited me.

(The scene has transitioned.)

SCENE 8

(The Parker family house. Late that night. RALPHIE is sitting on a stool with MOTHER and THE OLD MAN glowering over him while RANDY hides.)

MOTHER *(with a disciplinary tone).* Open up, Ralphie!

(She pops a bar of Lifebuoy soap into his mouth.)

JEAN *(with an air of sophistication).* I had become quite a connoisseur of soap. My personal preference was for Lux, but I found that Palmolive was quite piquant with just a touch of mellow smoothness … Lifebuoy, on the other hand …

RALPHIE *(with soap in his mouth).* Yuck.

MOTHER. All right. Where did you hear that word?

JEAN *(chuckles).* Now I'd heard that word at least twelve times a day from my old man. My father worked in profanity the way other artists might work in oils or clay. It was his true medium. But I chickened out.

MOTHER. Are you ready to tell me?

RALPHIE *(with soap still in mouth, indecipherable, reluctantly).* Schwartz.

(She takes the bar of soap out of RALPHIE's mouth.)

RALPHIE *(cont'd)*. Schwartz.

MOTHER. Oh, I see.

RALPHIE *(as MOTHER crams the soap back into his mouth)*. No! No! No! No!

(MOTHER goes to the phone and dials.

MRS. SCHWARTZ appears suddenly in a spotlight DR. She speaks nasally, answering with muffled words throughout the conversation.)

MRS. SCHWARTZ. Hello.

MOTHER. Hello, Mrs. Schwartz?

MRS. SCHWARTZ. Hello, Mrs. Parker, how are you?

MOTHER. I'm fine. Mrs. Schwartz, do you know what Ralph just said?

MRS. SCHWARTZ. I hear all the kids are saying "smartass" these days.

MOTHER. No. He said … *(Inaudible.)*

MRS. SCHWARTZ *(horrified)*. Oh no, not that!

MOTHER. Yes. That. And do you know where he heard it?

MRS. SCHWARTZ *(as if it were obvious)*. Probably from his father.

MOTHER *(offended)*. No. He heard it from your son!

MRS. SCHWARTZ *(with growing outrage)*. What? WHAT? WHAAAAAAT???

SCHWARTZ *(appearing beside her)*. Mom?

(As MRS. SCHWARTZ chases SCHWARTZ across the stage, we hear sounds of spanking and ad-libbed crying.)

SCHWARTZ *(cont'd)*. Ah! What'd I do? What'd I do? What'd I … ? *(They exit.)*

(#10: "Act I Finale")

(Suddenly, in a nightmare, the TOWNSPEOPLE pop out from behind the furniture, ghoulish and frightening.)

TOWNSPEOPLE.
GOODBYE RED RYDER

RALPHIE *(in despair)*.
MY DREAM IS *OVER*

TOWNSMAN SOLO.
DYING!

TOWNSWOMAN SOLO.
DEAD!

RALPHIE.
THERE'S NO WAY I'LL GET
THAT GUN WHEN I JUST SAID THAT WORD I SAID

RALPHIE & TOWNSPEOPLE.
IT'S A DISASTER

RALPHIE.
THERE'S NOTHING WORSE

TOWNSPEOPLE *(condescending and mean)*.
'CAUSE CHRISTMAS DOESN'T COME
FOR LITTLE KIDDIES WHO CURSE

RALPHIE.
THIS YEAR …

THE OLD MAN.
HOW 'BOUT A BIG LUMP OF COAL?

RALPHIE.
THIS YEAR …

MOTHER & RANDY.
NO PRETTY PRESENT FROM THE NORTH POLE!

ALL.
HA HA HA HA HA HA!

TOWNSMEN.
THERE'S NOT ENOUGH TIME!
THERE'S NOT ENOUGH TIME!

TOWNSWOMEN.
THERE'S NOT ENOUGH TIME!
THERE'S NOT ENOUGH TIME!

ALL *(spooky)*
AH!

RALPHIE.
YOU CAN'T SAY SOMETHING ROTTEN
'CAUSE IT ALL COMES DOWN TO CHRISTMAS
OH, THIS WON'T BE FORGOTTEN

ALL.
AND IT ALL COMES DOWN TO CHRISTMAS

RALPHIE *(overcome with anguish and desperation).*
I'VE GOT ONE SHOT
AND I'M WATCHING IT SLIP AWAY

(FARKUS and DILL enter, manhandling RALPHIE.)

FARKUS. C'mon, kid!

TOWNSPEOPLE.
AND NOW YOU HAVE TO
PAY THE PRICE BY

HAVING THE MOST
LOUSY, LONELY
DREADFUL, DREARY
HORRID, HELLISH
WRETCHED, RUINED
CHRISTMAS DAY!

(MOTHER dramatically inserts the soap back into RAL-PHIE's mouth as the characters onstage now resemble players in a grand opera.)

TOWNSPEOPLE *(cont'd).*
AAAAHH!!!

(For RALPHIE, the dream of getting the gun feels more distant than ever. Curtain.)

END OF ACT I

ACT II

(#11: "Entr'acte")

SCENE 1

(Mid "Entr'acte," we find JEAN in some semblance of his radio studio. Here, we briefly see him back in the radio broadcast before he once again becomes the active narrator of our story.)

JEAN. After the Lifebuoy soap debacle, my fate rested on a good grade from Miss Shields and keeping my nose clean till Christmas. But that would be severely challenged by an episode that would become legend at Warren G. Harding Elementary School.

(#11a: "Before Sticky Situation")

(The schoolyard. December 20, 1940.

The curtain opens to reveal the flagpole at C. KIDS are hanging around during recess. FLICK and SCHWARTZ enter the schoolyard near the flagpole.)

SCHWARTZ *(with an attitude).* All right, there's the flagpole. Why don't you put your tongue on it? I double dare you.

(#12: "Sticky Situation")

JEAN *(with hushed urgency).* The exact exchange and nuance of phrase in this ritual is very important.

FLICK. You kiddin'? Stick my tongue to that *stupid* pole? That's dumb.

SCHWARTZ. That's 'cause you know it'll stick.

FLICK. You're full of it.

SCHWARTZ. Oh, yeah?

FLICK. Yeah.

SCHWARTZ. Oh, yeah?

FLICK. Yeah.

SCHWARTZ. Oh, yeah?!

FLICK. Yeah!

SCHWARTZ. Well, I double *dog* dare you.

JEAN *(the tension builds).* Now it was serious. A double dog dare. What else was left but a triple-dare-you and the final coup de grâce of all dares—the sinister triple dog dare.

SCHWARTZ. I *triple* dog dare you.

(An audible gasp from all of the KIDS.)

JEAN. Schwartz created a slight breach of etiquette by skipping the triple dare and going right for the throat.

RALPHIE *(assessing the situation).*
    IT'S A STICKY SITUATION
    MAYBE FLICK IS JUST FULL OF HOT AIR

GIRL 1 & 2.
    BUT THERE'S A STANDARD EXPECTATION

RANDY & GIRL 3.
    HE'S GOT NO CHOICE BUT DOIN' THE DARE

RALPHIE.
    YOU CAN'T SKIP THE STANDARD TRIPLE
    FOR THE TRIPLE DOG DARE ATTACK

GIRL 1 & 2.
    BUT SCHWARTZ JUST UP AND SAID IT

GIRL 3 *(taking slight delight in this).*
    AND THERE AIN'T NO WAY OF TAKIN' IT BACK

RALPHIE.
  IT'S A STICKY, STICKY, STICKY SITUATION

(FLICK and SCHWARTZ are now inches from the flagpole. The other KIDS look on with anxious anticipation.)

FLICK. All right. All right.

SCHWARTZ. Well, go on, smartass, and do it.

FLICK *(defensive, confident)*. I'm goin', I'm goin'.

JEAN. Flick's spine stiffened. His lips curled in a defiant sneer. There was no going back now.

(FLICK plants his tongue on the pole.)

FLICK *(tongue-tied, with a lisp)*. This is nothin'. *(Slowly realizing ... gradually turning hysterical.)* Stuck ... stuck ... stuck? I'm stuck!

MARY BETH. What did he say?

SCHWARTZ *(sheer astonishment)*. Jeez, it really worked!

RALPHIE. Schwartz's old man was right!

SCHWARTZ. Told ya!

(The school bell rings. The KIDS begin inching away toward the school, unsure of how to deal with the quandary they find themselves in.)

FLICK *(with his tongue stuck, he attempts to speak)*. —Hey fellas, help me, come on—

SCHWARTZ. What are we going to do?

RALPHIE *(inching away toward the school, in somewhat of a panic)*. The bell rang. We've gotta go back in.

SCHWARTZ *(pointing to FLICK)*. But what are we going to do?

JEAN. The horns of a dilemma. Good little boys who were on time for class got what they asked for on Christmas, even

BB guns. But bad little boys who got caught triple dog dar-
ing their friends to stick their tongues to a flagpole? Well,
what would *you* do?

RALPHIE *(a beat. Then, straightforward, they have but one
choice)*. Let's go!

SCHWARTZ. Come on!

JEAN. Yeah, let's get out of here!

(All KIDS abandon FLICK and run back to school.)

FLICK *(calling after them with a thick lisp by now)*. Don't
leave me. Come back—come back!
   (With his tongue still stuck to the pole.)
   IT'S A STICKY, STICKY, STICKY SITUATION

JEAN. As we bolted back to the classroom from recess leav-
ing poor Flick fastened to the flagpole, only one lingering
thought was on my mind—we had to get our themes back
today. It was the last day before Christmas vacation.

*(The KIDS are now in the classroom. MISS SHIELDS en-
ters and begins to count the students.)*

MISS SHIELDS. Esther Jane … Ralphie … Flick … Where's
Flick? Has anyone seen Flick? He was at recess, wasn't
he? Ralphie, do you know where Flick is?

*(RALPHIE looks around blankly, as though he has no idea
who she's talking about.)*

JEAN *(clueless)*. Flick? Flick who?

ALL KIDS *(except FLICK)*.
   IT'S A STICKY SITUATION
   IN THE THICK OF THIS CRAZY EVENT

SCHWARTZ.
SHOULD YOU TRY A LIE?

ALL KIDS *(except FLICK)*.
AN EXPLANATION OF WHERE FLICK
MIGHT COULD HAVE POSSIBLY WENT

RALPHIE. He ran away.

SCHWARTZ. He forgot his lunch.

MARY BETH. He died.

KIDS 1.
YOU JUST SIT, DON'T DARE ADMIT IT

KIDS 2.
IF YOU'RE CAUGHT, THEY MIGHT HAUL YOU TO JAIL

ALL KIDS.
AND IN JAIL, THEY DON'T HAVE CHRISTMAS

ALL GIRLS *(heartbroken)*.
AND SANTA DOESN'T ANSWER YOUR MAIL

ALL KIDS.
IT'S A STICKY, STICKY, STICKY
STICKY, STICKY, STICKY
STICKY, STICKY, STICKY SITUATION

MISS SHIELDS *(sternly)*. I said! Has anyone seen Flick?

(ESTHER JANE meekly raises her hand.)

MISS SHIELDS *(cont'd)*. Yes, Esther Jane.

(ESTHER JANE reluctantly points to the window, through which we can see poor FLICK still struggling to loosen himself from the flagpole. MISS SHIELDS looks outside and sees FLICK.)

MISS SHIELDS *(cont'd, practically fainting at the sight of it).*
Oh, my Lord!

(As our focus shifts back outside, a POLICEMAN, FIRE-MAN, DOCTOR, NURSE and FLICK'S MOTHER enter to try and save FLICK.)

POLICEMAN & DOCTOR *(in a rush, but matter-of-fact).*
IT'S A STICKY SITUATION

POLICEMAN.
GOTTA QUICKLY GET THE KID TO RELAX

FLICK.
STICKY, STICKY!

DOCTOR.
HE'LL NEED IMMEDIATE HYDRATION

FIREMAN *(suddenly brandishing an ax).*
AND IF THAT DON'T WORK, I'LL BREAK OUT THE AX!

FLICK'S MOM. Aaaahhhh!! That's my son!! *(Screams a bloodcurdling scream.)*

FLICK. *(still with a lisp, giving his account of the events.)*
JUST A LICK
MY TONGUE GOT STICKY
AND IT STARTED SWELLING OUT OF CONTROL

ALL ADULTS *(perhaps a bit overly dramatic).*
HE COULD DIE RIGHT HERE AT RECESS
UNLESS WE PRY HIM OFFA THAT POLE!

IT'S A—

ALL ADULTS & KIDS.
STICKY, STICKY, STICKY

(Using hot water to thaw his tongue, they attempt to pull him from the pole.)

FLICK.   ADULTS & KIDS.
  OW!   *OOH!*

ALL ADULTS & KIDS.
  STICKY, STICKY, STICKY

(They attempt once again to pull him from the pole.)

FLICK.   ADULTS & KIDS.
  OW!   *OOH!*

ALL ADULTS & KIDS.
  STICKY, STICKY, STICKY SITUATION

FLICK.   ADULTS & KIDS.
  OW! OW!   *OOH!*

(They have successfully removed FLICK from the pole.)

FLICK. Sthlun uv a— *(A lisped version of "son of a ___ .")*

(The DOCTOR or FIREMAN or POLICEMAN covers his mouth just in time so we don't hear the word. Music: Button.)

(#12a: "Sticky Situation" [Playoff])

(FLICK'S MOM leads him away, scolding him. The POLICEMAN, FIREMAN, DOCTOR and NURSE exit. MISS SHIELDS returns to the classroom.)

MISS SHIELDS *(didactic)*. Now I know some of you put Flick up to this. But those who did know their blame. And I'm sure the guilt is far worse than any punishment you might receive. Don't you feel terrible? Don't you feel remorse … for what you have done?

JEAN *(chuckling)*. Adults love to say things like that. But kids know better. We know darn well it was always better not to get caught.

(FLICK enters the classroom, sulking, and sits in his chair. Several giggles are heard.)

MISS SHIELDS. Well, that's all I'm going to say about poor Flick. *(Shifting topics.)* All right, class, I have your Christmas themes for you. *(She picks the themes up from her desk and begins to pass them out.)*

JEAN *(relieved)*. At last!

MISS SHIELDS. I'm pleased. They were generally pretty good, except for the margins. Look at your paper only. No talking now.

(She finally hands RALPHIE his theme. He holds it without opening it, anticipating an impressively high grade.)

JEAN. I held my breath as I stared at the paper. I imagined Miss Shields was restraining her verbal praise of my theme in deference to the ordinary intelligence of my classmates.

(The KIDS look at one another's papers and generally congratulate one another on what seems to be uniformly good grades.)

JEAN *(cont'd)*. I was sure the multiple pluses were fairly dripping to the floor.

(RALPHIE looks at his paper.)

JEAN *(cont'd, shock and anger)*. But there was only one plus.

RALPHIE *(outraged)*. C-plus?

(Instantly, MISS SHIELDS assumes the demeanor of a menacing 1930's gun moll or nightclub singer.)

MISS SHIELDS *(delighting in his misfortune)*. Ha, ha, ha, ha! C-plus!

JEAN. Along with a note at the bottom.

MISS SHIELDS *(puffing a cigar, she casually seals his fate)*. P.S. You'll shoot your eye out!

RALPHIE & JEAN. Oh, noooo!

MISS SHIELDS. Take him away, boys!

(#12b: "To the Nightclub")

SCENE 2

(A 1930s kid gangster fantasy at a speakeasy.

FARKUS and DILL enter dressed as dancing 1930's gang-sters, manhandling and kidnapping RALPHIE as all the KIDS and MISS SHIELDS exit and the classroom disappears.)

FARKUS & DILL *(in their best mobster/gangster voices)*.
      C-PLUS! C-PLUS!
      NOT AN A, NOT A B
      BUT A C-PLUS!

RALPHIE *(trying to escape their clutches with no success)*.
      HEY!

(A small cutout getaway car enters. DILL is driving. FARKUS shoves RALPHIE into the car and it speeds away. They bounce along on the joy ride until they arrive at their destination.)

FARKUS & DILL *(cont'd, taunting)*.
      THE BOSS ISN'T HAPPY
      SHE ISN'T IMPRESSED
      YOUR REPORT CAME UP SHORT
      SO YOU FAILED THE TEST
      HEY!

RALPHIE, YOU'RE DONE
THAT'S A FACT
SO, GIVE UP THE GUN
OR YOU'RE GONNA GET WHACKED

(They arrive at a small dark door with the word "SPEAKEZY" written on it. The peephole on the door slides open. SCHWARTZ is the gatekeeper.)

FARKUS *(using the secret code word).*
　　'SALRIGHT?

SCHWARTZ.
　　'SALRIGHT.

(They have arrived at the "SPEAKEZY" cabaret. All the kids enter, dressed as mobsters and gun molls with tap shoes.)

GIRLS *(á lá nightclub showgirls).*
　　MEET THE GAL WHO MAKES THE GRADE
　　HERE SHE COMES TO SERENADE
　　WHO CAN FACE THE POWER SHE WIELDS?

FLICK *(in his best announcer voice).*
　　LADIES AND GENTLEMEN
　　MISS SHIELDS!

(Applause from the KIDS as MISS SHIELDS enters in '30s glamour garb. They are seated at cabaret tables, ready to take in the performance. During the number, MISS SHIELDS taps and sings, entertaining the crowd while teasing and taunting RALPIIIE.)

(#13: "You'll Shoot Your Eye Out!")

MISS SHIELDS.
　　YOUR THEME WAS GOOD FOR A LAUGH
　　YOU'LL SHOOT YOUR EYE OUT

YOU'RE BARELY NINE AND A HALF!
YOU'LL SHOOT YOUR EYE OUT

SEEMS LIKE YOUR BIG DREAMS
OUGHTA BE LEFT ON THE SHELF
WHY AIM FOR THE SKY?
IF YOU'RE NOT CAREFUL, KID
YOU'LL SHOOT YOURSELF!

I HATE TO SPOIL THE FUN
WITH "YOU'LL SHOOT YOUR EYE OUT"
BUT HON, START KISSIN' THAT GUN GOODBYE

WELL, SHOOT, IT'S CUTE THAT YOU DESIRE IT
(Á lá Jimmy Durante.)
BUT THE MOMENT THAT YOU FIRE IT
YOU'LL SHOOT YOUR EYE OUT!

I'M SURE YOU'RE SICK OF MY SPIEL, BUT
(Letting loose.)
A-DA-BA-DA-BA-DOO
YOU'LL SHOOT YOUR EYE OUT!
AND THOUGH YOU GAVE IT A REAL GOOD TRY
I BET THAT YOU'D REGRET LETTIN' A
LITTLE BULLET CRACK YOUR RETINA
YOU'LL SHOOT YOUR EYE OUT!

(Tap dance section. The gangster KIDS become involved in the number.)

GIRLS *(like whiny showgirls).*
YOU'LL SHOOT YOUR EYE OUT

(Tap dance section. Along with full choreography for the group, MISS SHIELDS and TAP SPECIALTY BOY have a tap dance-off, followed by a solo virtuoso improv section by the TAP SPECIALTY BOY. RALPHIE is overwhelmed by all of it.)

KIDS.
> *HEY! HEY!*
> *HEY! HEY!*
> *HEY! HEY!*

(Dance section. MISS SHIELDS and the KIDS use their dance to taunt RALPHIE, who is watching in disbelief.)

MISS SHIELDS.
> HERE'S TO THE DUNCE OF THE CLASS

GIRLS *(again, the showgirls)*.
> YOU'LL SHOOT YOUR EYE OUT!

MISS SHIELDS.
> HEY, RALPH, WE'RE RAISIN' OUR GLASSES HIGH!
>
> NOW I CAN TELL THIS TUNE'S DEPRESSIN' YOU
> BUT I'M SPELLING OUT A LESSON YOU
> NEED TO BE TAUGHT
> IT'S GOTTA GET THROUGH

KIDS.
> THEY WONT GIVE A GUN TO A SHRIMP LIKE YOU

MISS SHIELDS.
> IT'S TIME TO GIVE UP
> 'CAUSE TEACHER KNOWS BEST

KIDS.
> YOU'RE THE WIMPIEST KID
> IN THE WHOLE MIDWEST

MISS SHIELDS.
> YOU CAN CRY
> YOU CAN POUT
> I'M TELLING YOU, KID
> THAT THERE'S NO DOUBT
>
> YOU'LL SHOOT YOUR EYE OUT!

(Big tap finish! RALPHIE is defeated. The KIDS, in celebration, move off to the next speakeasy. MISS SHIELDS, winded, struggles to keep up.)

MISS SHIELDS *(calling offstage)*. Yeah, I'm comin'! Call me a cab!

(#13a: "You'll Shoot Your Eye Out!" [Playoff])

SCENE 3

(A path from school, immediately following.

After the song, RALPHIE, alone and downcast, is found sitting outside in the snow. FARKUS and DILL sneak up on him. He tries to get away, but they trip him. RANDY enters to find his brother on the ground.)

FARKUS *(threatening)*. Come here, jerk! … Hey, Parker, when I tell you to come here, you better come here.

DILL *(measured menacing tones, as if compensating for his size)*. Better do what he says, Ralphie boy!

(JEAN enters.)

JEAN. Ah, the venomous vipers of the jungle appear once again.

RANDY *(afraid)*. Come on, Ralphie, let's run home.

JEAN. But sometimes in this wild wilderness, there emerges a small red demon, a beady-eyed carnivore, an insane little beast that, on rare occasion, inhabits us all.

FARKUS. Come on, fat mess. What, you goin' to cry?

DILL. You goin' to cry?

FARKUS. Come on cry! Cry baby! Cry!

DILL. Cry baby!

FARKUS *(louder)*. Cry!

DILL *(even louder)*. Cry!

FARKUS *(louder still)*. Cry!

(#13b: "The Fight")

(During JEAN's speech, we see the rage boil and well up within RALPHIE as he prepares to attack. He has reached his breaking point.)

JEAN. And on that day, at that moment, the demon not only inhabited me, it consumed me. It possessed me. I threw myself at the tormentor with a strength I'd never known.

RALPHIE *(losing all control and jumping onto FARKUS as he squeals a high-pitched, almost girlish squeal)*. AHHH-HH!!! *(He goes into a full-on faux-profanity rage.)* Gol-buster balfaddle fulfuse flappermap!

(In an exaggerated, heightened manner, FARKUS falls to the ground, and RALPHIE punches and smacks him. FARKUS groans and cries.)

RANDY. Ralphie, stop it! You're going to kill him.

RALPHIE *(continuing the choreographed fight)*. Stick-a-lick-a, mac-a-lack-a!

DILL. Hey! Get off of him!

(RALPHIE sucker-punches DILL.)

RANDY *(quickly, running offstage)*. Mom! Mom! You gotta come quick!

(Other KIDS enter and, mesmerized, watch the fight.)

RALPHIE *(almost delighting in the profanity and violence. Broad gestures, over the top)*. Confaluted frazzle-baster pena-lotta corn doodle dooooo!

(He continues the "profanity" under JEAN's line.)

JEAN. By now, I was beyond profanity. I was speaking in tongues!

RALPHIE *(stylized he-man warrior celebration. He is conquering his foe)*. He-bee, je-bee! Arkanoble! Umlay, umlay, umlay!

(RALPHIE is still clobbering FARKUS as MOTHER enters, rushing on, with RANDY close behind.)

RALPHIE *(cont'd.)* Glockenspeilia cheriberium! Eglottal! Eglottal! Eglottal! *(With a finishing blow, he clobbers FARKUS.)* Splid!

MOTHER *(overlapping with RALPHIE)*. Ralphie! Stop it! Stop it!

(She tries to pull RALPHIE off of FARKUS, then implores the gathered KIDS.)

MOTHER *(cont'd)*. Somebody ... boys! Help me get him off.

(Two or three of the KIDS help MOTHER pull RALPHIE from the defeated FARKUS who, along with RALPHIE, is crying.)

SCHWARTZ. Way to go, Parker!

GIRL 1. Hooray for Ralphie!

(The KIDS break into a cheer.)

ALL KIDS.
   WHEN YOU'RE A WIMP
   YOU PATIENTLY WAIT FOR THE DAY ...
   WHEN THE TABLES HAVE TURNED
   AND YOU'RE MAKIN' 'EM PAY

MOTHER *(interrupting them)*. Kids! Now stop that.

(DILL comes to the aid of FARKUS and helps him up. Barely able to stand, FARKUS is dragged off by DILL as they exit.)

FLICK *(his tongue still in bandages from the flagpole accident)*. But that was Scut Farkus. He showed Scut Farkus who's boss!

MOTHER. I don't care about Scut Farkus.

MARY BETH. He's a big bully!

MOTHER. It makes no difference!

(MOTHER speaks as she and RANDY help RALPHIE up.)

MOTHER *(cont'd, forcefully)*. Now all of you go home. *(A moment later, smiling weakly.)* And have a merry Christmas.

(She picks up RALPHIE's glasses that have fallen to the ground and puts them in her pocket.

The KIDS start to leave, all overlapping. MOTHER gathers a crying RALPHIE and heads home as RANDY follows.)

(#14: "Just Like That")

GIRL 1. Do you believe that?

GIRL 2. Ralphie beat the stuffing out of Scut Farkus …

SCHWARTZ. I never thought it would happen. Especially by Parker.

ESTHER JANE. He tore right into him.

MARY BETH. I think that's the last we'll see of Farkus for a while … and Dill, too …

(The KIDS ad-lib as they exit.)

JEAN *(in momentary celebration)*. I had won!

(The Parker family house comes into view as MOTHER comforts RALPHIE on the way to the house.)

MOTHER. Shh … shh …

JEAN. I had pummeled Farkus and sent Dill running for the hills.

MOTHER. Ralphie … Ralphie.

JEAN. But I had also disappointed my mother, losing any chance of procuring the coveted Christmas gift.

MOTHER. Settle down, Ralphie. Just settle down …

JEAN *(realizing what's to come)*. Surely the fight and the profanity had sealed my fate, especially when the old man found out.

(RALPHIE, MOTHER and JEAN have entered the house. RANDY hides under the sink.)

SCENE 4

(The Parker family house. Immediately afterward.

MOTHER, comforting RALPHIE, who is sobbing, and RAN-DY enter the living room. RANDY hides under the sink.)

MOTHER. Hey, hey, hey. It's OK. You're gonna be all right …

(MOTHER, always practical and straightforward, comforts RALPHIE.)

CATCH YOUR BREATH AND LOOK AROUND
THERE'S NO MONSTER WAITING BY
NOTHING'S CRUMBLING TO THE GROUND
NOTHING'S TUMBLING FROM THE SKY

NOTICE HOW THE WORLD KEEPS TURNING
LIFE GOES ON
A MOMENT COMES
A MOMENT GOES
AND JUST LIKE THAT
THE MOMENT'S GONE

(RALPHIE is still upset, whimpers.)

IF YOU SLIP AND SCRAPE YOUR KNEE
THINK IT'S NEVER GONNA HEAL
IN A DAY OR TWO YOU'LL SEE
IT'S JUST NOT THAT BIG A DEAL

AND YOU'RE BACK TO JUMPING, LAUGHING
YOU'VE MOVED ON

THE MOMENT COMES
THE MOMENT GOES
AND JUST LIKE THAT
THE MOMENT'S GONE

(RALPHIE seems to gain control, then bursts into tears again.)

MOTHER *(cont'd)*. Now, Ralphie, go to your room and lie down.

(RALPHIE slowly goes upstairs and exits into his bedroom. RANDY is heard whimpering. MOTHER opens the door beneath the sink.)

MOTHER *(cont'd, sweetly)*. Randy? Hi. Can I come in? What's the matter? Whatcha crying for?

RANDY *(whimpering)*. Daddy's gonna kill Ralphie! *(Lets out a wail.)*

MOTHER *(almost amused by his sweet innocence)*. No, he's not. I promise you Daddy is not going to kill anyone. Want some milk?

RANDY *(nodding his head)*. Uh-huh.

MOTHER. You would? *(She hands him a glass of milk, which he takes, immediately shutting the cupboard door.)* Oh, Randy …

(In a moment to herself)

ALL THESE CRAZY MOMENTS
FLICKER PAST
AND THEY'RE GONE
CRAZY, MESSY MOMENTS
YET YOU TRY
TO HOLD ON.

(She suddenly makes this realization. It's as true for her children as it is for her.)

'CAUSE THEY PASS YOU IN AN INSTANT
PASS YOU BY SO FAST

DON'T FORGET TO REMEMBER
THESE MOMENTS NEVER LAST

(Distant sounds of the BUMPUS HOUNDS barking are heard. Panicked, RALPHIE emerges from his room and trembles with fear.)

JEAN *(with dread)*. Oh no! The old man was home. I'd be drawn and quartered when he found out about the fight.

THE OLD MAN *(entering)*. Get away, you mangy malfroggin' mutts! Shoo! Git! Bumpus! Keep your slobberin' hounds outta my yard!

(RALPHIE slowly descends the stairs.)

MOTHER. Hello, dear. How was your day?

THE OLD MAN *(grumbling)*. Aw, the Bears say they're going to start Bulholtz this Sunday. The worst quarterback in the—*(Sees RALPHIE. Instant anger.)* Where's your glasses? Did you lose your glasses again?

MOTHER *(quickly rescuing RALPHIE, who's frozen in fear)*. Ralphie, here's your glasses.

(MOTHER takes the glasses from her pocket and goes to RALPHIE. She smoothly invents an excuse for him)

MOTHER *(cont'd.)* You left them on the radio. Don't you do that again.

(RALPHIE takes the glasses, slightly relieved but still nervous. THE OLD MAN, RALPHIE and RANDY sit at the table.)

THE OLD MAN. So, what happened today?

MOTHER *(pauses, then casually offers as she continues with kitchen chores)*. Oh, Ralphie got into a fight.

(RALPHIE stiffens.)

THE OLD MAN *(ready to blow a fuse)*. Fight? What kind of fight?

(RALPHIE is now paralyzed with fear.)

MOTHER. Oh, it was … *(Softening.)* Oh, you know how boys are … It wasn't much. I gave him a talking to … *(Effortlessly changing the subject, she completely bypasses any further discussion of the fight.)* You say the Bears are starting Bulholtz this Sunday?

THE OLD MAN *(pauses, somewhat surprised)*. Yeah. Yeah, I didn't know you paid attention to—

MOTHER. Why don't you go to the game? Take Ralphie with you.

(MOTHER makes eye contact with a much-relieved RALPHIE.)

THE OLD MAN *(offhand)*. Maybe I will. *(More convincingly.)* Maybe I will … *(Even showing a hint of affection toward RALPHIE.)* Though we'll probably freeze our keesters off. That reminds me. I need to put some more antifreeze in the Olds. *(He exits.)*

JEAN *(astonished)*. I couldn't believe my ears. Perhaps I was not about to be destroyed after all.

(RALPHIE looks at his mother, a bit overwhelmed by the miracle she has just pulled off.)

MOTHER.
　　NOTICE HOW THE WORLD KEEPS TURNING
　　LIFE GOES ON

JEAN. From then on, things were different between me and my mother.

(Giving both her boys a final bit of comfort.)

MOTHER.
> AND JUST LIKE THAT
> THE MOMENT'S GONE

JEAN. As my gloom slowly lifted, I began to realize that all was not lost. There was one last hope,

(#14a: "Red Ryder [Reprise #1] & At Higbee's")

JEAN *(cont'd)*. Right downtown at Higbee's Department Store.

RALPHIE *(hopeful)*.
> GOTTA FIND A WAY TO GET TO SANTA
> TELL HIM CLEARLY
> AND HE'LL HEAR ME
> HE'S THE ONE
> GET THE RED RYDER CARBINE-ACTION BB GUN

SCENE 5

(Santa's station at Higbee's Department Store. Christmas Eve. The department store ELVES are finishing a performance of their hourly Christmas show. They are overly enthusiastic, over-the-top, saccharinely sweet, yet miserable being there.)

ELVES *(with forced, manic enthusiasm)*.
> CATCH THE SEASON SPIRIT AT HIGBEE'S.

FEMALE CHIEF ELF *(a bit rough)*.
> HIGBEE'S!

ELVES.
> CHRISTMAS CHEER IS HERE TO STAY.
> WE'VE STOCKED THE SHELVES WITH TONS OF TOYS

TO TAKE YOUR BREATH AWAY.
(Completely winded, they gasp for breath.)
HAH! HAH! HAH!
COME EXPLORE ALL THAT AND MORE AT—

ELF 1.
    H—

ELF 2.
    I—

ELF 3.
    G—

ELF 4.
    B—

ELF 5.
    E—

ELF 6.
    E—

FEMALE CHIEF ELF.
    APOSTROPHE—

ELF 8.
    S!

ELVES.
    HIGBEE'S STORE TODAY!

(A big finish. FEMALE CHIEF ELF struggles to come out of a split.)

FEMALE CHIEF ELF. Ow! Ow! Ow!

(#15: "Up on Santa's Lap")

(Revealed is a steep, narrow stairway leading to the top of a platform that is highly decorated in the spirit of the season. A somewhat sad and weary SANTA, flanked by two very impatient CHIEF ELVES, sits at the top. At the side of the platform is a long playground-type slide leading from the top to the bottom. A line of screaming, restless KIDS seems to stretch and snake for miles. As the scene opens, the two CHIEF ELVES, who aren't particularly gentle with the KIDS, lift a KID off of SANTA's lap and send him/her down the slide. MARY BETH climbs up to SANTA.)

FEMALE CHIEF ELF. Nobody gets to see Santa till you shut up!

SANTA *(ready to be done for the day)*.
    HOP ON MY KNEE, KID

MARY BETH *(snotty and perturbed)* . Well it's about time—

SANTA.
    WHAT'LL IT BE, KID?

MARY BETH. *(producing a long scroll-like wishlist)* Tinker-toys, X-ray glasses— *(She continues to pantomime reading her list to SANTA.)*

SANTA.
    I'M ENDIN' MY SHIFT
    SO ONLY ONE GIFT
    (His mind wanders.)
    AND WHY IS THIS SUIT SO TIGHT?
    I'M GONNA CHAFE ALL NIGHT

MARY BETH *(still aggressively reading from her list)*. A teddy bear, a Monopoly set—

SANTA.
    I GET AN EARFUL

MARY BETH. A decoder pin, a new pair of gloves—

SANTA.
    GOTTA BE CHEERFUL!

MARY BETH *(emphatic and demanding with this last one)*.
    Oh! And a collie named Fluffy!

SANTA.
    OH, GIMME A BREAK!
    HOW LONG CAN I TAKE THIS CRAP?!

    (He sends MARY BETH down the slide.)

MARY BETH *(sliding down)*. Aaaahhhh!!!

    (The ELVES shuffle NANCY up to see SANTA. She climbs up and whispers in his ear.)

SANTA.
    UP ON SANTA'S LAP!
    LITTLE NANCY WANTS A NEW TOY TRAIN

NANCY *(maniacally mimicking the gift she desires)*.
    WOO! WOO!

SANTA.
    LITTLE NANCY'S DRIVIN' ME INSANE

ELVES *(unenthused)*.
    WOO! WOO!

SANTA.
    AIN'T THAT A LOVELY CHRISTMAS MOB
    I HATE MY JOB
    HEY!

(SANTA launches NANCY down the slide.)

SANTA *(cont'd)*.
    UP ON SANTA'S LAP!
    HIGBEE'S GOTTA PAY ME OVERTIME

(A boy wearing goggles, GOGGLES KID, climbs up to SANTA. He is very bizarre, a bit off.)

SANTA *(cont'd)*.
    FOR THE LITTLE FREAKS WHO COME TO CLIMB
    ON SANTA'S LAP.

GOGGLES KID *(eccentric, breathing heavily)*. I like you, Santa ... I like you, Santa ... *(He sighs as he relieves himself in ecstasy.)*

SANTA. Ew, he's a wet one! Someone get him off me and get me a towel!

GOGGLES KID. Santa! Santa! *(He is thrown down the slide.)*

(We focus on the eager and antsy KIDS still waiting in line, each one a bit quirkier than the one before)

KID 1.
    WHAT WILL I TELL HIM?

KID 2.
    CAN'T WAIT TO SMELL HIM

RANDY.
    WHAT IS HE LIKE?

KID 3 *(harassing an ELF)*.
    I WANT A NEW BIKE
    BUT HOW SHOULD I ASK FOR IT?

RALPHIE *(impatient)*.
    COULD YOU MOVE UP A BIT?

(SANTA takes a drink from a flask.)

KID 4.
>WHAT IS HE THINKING?

SANTA *(sloppy)*. Meeerrrryyy Christmassss …

KID 5.
>WHAT IS HE DRINKING?

ALL KIDS.
>WHO KNOWS WHAT HE MIGHT
>PULL OUTTA THAT BRIGHT RED CAP?

(SANTA sends another KID down the slide as the ELVES bring up the next victim.)

FEMALE CHIEF ELF *(hostile)*. Get movin', kid!
MALE CHIEF ELF *(grumpy)*. You had your turn!
KID 6 *(going down the slide)*. Heeeeeeeeyyyyyy!

SANTA, KIDS & ELVES.
>UP ON SANTA'S LAP

KIDS & ELVES.
>HE CAN MAKE YOUR CHRISTMAS DREAMS COME
>   TRUE.

SANTA *(mockingly)*.
>WHICH IS SOMETHING THAT I RARELY DO
>*HO! HO!*

SANTA, ELVES & KIDS.
>ON SANTA'S LAP!

(Another KID is shoved down the slide.)

SANTA. Neeeexxxxtttt! *(Takes another drink.)*

ELVES *(nasal, grating)*.
> SEE THE BEASTLY BRATS BEFORE US
> STRETCHING MILES THROUGH THE AISLES OF THE
>   STORE
> PLEADING, "SANTA, DON'T IGNORE US NOW"

FEMALE CHIEF ELF.
> WHO CARES IF THEY'RE STUCK IN LINE?

SANTA.
> THERE'S NO WAY I'LL STAY PAST NINE

SANTA & ELVES.
> *HA! HA! HA! HA!*
> *HO! HO! HO! HO!*

(SANTA has become much more intoxicated.)

JEAN *(eager to log his request)*. Finally, after two eons and fifty-nine minutes, the Parker boys were next in line to climb Mount Olympus.

(RANDY climbs up to SANTA.)

SANTA & ELVES.
> UP ON SANTA'S LAP

(RANDY, comes face-to-face with SANTA and, after a beat, lets out one long, blood-curdling scream.)

RANDY *(going down the slide)*. AAHHHHH!!!!

(He runs offstage, past the waiting arms of MOTHER and THE OLD MAN, screaming all the way. RALPHIE climbs up to SANTA.)

ELVES.
> UP ON SANTA'S LAP!

(Note: The following eight lines, with the exception of JEAN's dialogue, may be delivered in slow motion and with an echo effect. RALPHIE views this moment in a hazy, qua-si-nightmarish way.)

SANTA. What's your name, little boy?

MALE CHIEF ELF. Come on, kid.

FEMALE CHIEF ELF. It's nearly nine. The store's closing.

SANTA. What do you want for Christmas?

JEAN. My mind had gone blank. I was blowing it. Blowing it.

MALE CHIEF ELF. Hurry up, kid.

FEMALE CHIEF ELF. Come on.

SANTA. What about a nice football?

JEAN. Football? Football? What's a football? Without con-scious will, my voice squeaked out—

RALPHIE *(mindlessly, in a haze)*. Football.

SANTA *(back to real time)*. OK, get him outta here.

(JEAN speaks as RALPHIE is being pushed down the slide.)

JEAN. A football? Oh, no. What was I doing? Wake up, stu-pid, wake up!

RALPHIE *(stopping himself mid-slide, climbing back up)*. No! No! I want an official Red Ryder carbine-action 200-shot Range Model air rifle! *(He shoots a wink and a smile to the audience, self-satisfied.)*

SANTA. You'll shoot your eye out, kid. Ho! Ho! Ho!

(With his boot, SANTA pushes RALPHIE, who is devastat-ed, down the slide.)

RALPHIE *(going down the slide)*. NOOOOOOOO!

SANTA & ELVES.
     UP ON SANTA'S LAP

MALE CHIEF ELF *(to RALPHIE)*.
    KINDA CRUMMY THAT YOU GOT THE BOOT

FEMALE CHIEF ELF.
    NOW WE'RE CLOSING AND YOU HAFTA SCOOT

ELVES *(mocking RALPHIE)*. Have a nice Christmas!

(Preparing to leave for the night, SANTA and ELVES send RALPHIE off in showy yet dismissive fashion).

SANTA & ELVES.
    UP ON SANTA'S LAP

ELVES.
    SAD TO SAY THAT'S ALL THE TIME WE'VE GOT

SANTA
    'CAUSE YOU ONLY EVER GET ONE SHOT

MALE ELVES.
    YOU ONLY GET ONE SHOT

FEMALE ELVES.
    YOU ONLY GET ONE SHOT

SANTA.
    ON SANTA'S LAP!

FEMALE ELVES.
    ON SANTA'S LAP!

MALE ELVES.
    ON SANTA'S LAP!

ALL.
    HO! HO! HO! HO!

(SANTA and the ELVES exit, perhaps ready to blow off some steam. RALPHIE, somewhat shaken, is comforted by JEAN.)

(#15a: "Up on Santa's Lap [Playoff] & Transition to the Parker House")

JEAN. Despite my near debacle with Santa and the elves at Higbee's, I *had* managed to at least log my air rifle request with the big man. Who knows—maybe I'd get the air rifle *and* a football. It was Christmas Eve. I had renewed reason for optimism. But, of course, that's always the moment when life plays tricks on you. Cruel, unexpected tricks.

SCENE 6

(The Parker family house. Christmas Eve. In low light, we hear sounds of THE OLD MAN grumbling and working on the furnace in the basement as MOTHER is rearranging decorations in the window. Suddenly, we hear crashing sounds. The lights come up to reveal MOTHER and the broken leg lamp on the floor.)

THE OLD MAN *(from offstage)*. What broke?

(RALPHIE and RANDY retreat into hiding, fearing what may come next. THE OLD MAN emerges from the cellar.)

THE OLD MAN *(cont'd)*. What happened? What broke?

JEAN. At that moment, the old man knew. A thing he'd feared from the very first day had come to pass.

MOTHER *(softly, but overly dramatic)*. The lamp.

(THE OLD MAN is devastated. He rushes to the lamp. RALPHIE has come out of his room, and RANDY has now poked his head out of the below-the-sink door. THE OLD MAN drops to the floor beside the broken lamp.)

MOTHER *(cont'd)*. I—I don't know what happened. I was just—setting out the candles … and … and …

THE OLD MAN *(after a long pause, in measured tones)*. You were always jealous of that lamp.

MOTHER *(incredulous)*. Jealous? Of a plastic leg?

THE OLD MAN *(the tension is mounting)*. You were jealous because I won!

MOTHER. That's ridiculous! Jealous! Jealous of what? *(She can't hold back any longer.)* That was the ugliest lamp I ever saw.

(A long pause.)

THE OLD MAN *(standing, staring at her with indignation)*. Get the glue.

MOTHER. We're out of glue.

THE OLD MAN *(shudders with rage)*. Aha! You ran out of glue on purpose.

MOTHER. Randy used it up on a school project. I haven't had a chance to buy some more.

THE OLD MAN *(with formality and bristling dignity)*. Then I shall buy some more.

MOTHER. At six o'clock on Christmas Eve?

THE OLD MAN. Oh, I'll find some—somewhere. *(Gets his coat and starts to leave).* And—don't—touch—that—lamp. *(Quickly.)* Don't touch that lamp. *(Marches out the door, then returns.)* Not a finger.

MOTHER *(hurt)*. I've never wanted to touch that lamp.

THE OLD MAN *(not letting up)*. Well, you certainly touched it tonight, didn't you?! *(He exits in a huff.)*

MOTHER *(after a moment, angry and near tears, calling offstage)*. Boys, I'm going next door to Mrs. Cartwright's for a little while. Randy, your dinner is still on the table. You're the only one who didn't finish eating.

*(She grabs her coat and exits. Slowly, RALPHIE and RAN-
DY enter. They creep over and survey the damage.)*

JEAN. Nothing like this had ever happened before.

RANDY *(in awe of the mess)*. Wow.

(#16: "Before The Old Man Comes Home")

JEAN. I suddenly had an idea that might pay dividends on
Christmas morning—*if* it worked.

RALPHIE. Maybe we can do something.

RANDY. What?

RALPHIE.
GRAB THAT PIECE
FROM THE FLOOR
FIX IT UP
LIKE BEFORE
TAKE THE KNEE
WAIT, LIFT IT HIGHER
(He plugs in the leg lamp.)

RANDY.
HE'LL FORGET THAT IT BROKE

RALPHIE.
THERE WE GO

(The electrical outlet begins to emit smoke.)

RANDY *(frightened)*.
IS THAT SMOKE?

RALPHIE.
OH MY GOSH!

RANDY.
IT SMELLS LIKE FIRE!

RALPHIE & RANDY.
AH!

(The BOYS quickly jump away from the lamp, pulling the cord from the outlet.)

RALPHIE.
HERE, TAKE THE HEEL OF THE SHOE

RANDY *(giving up)*.
WE'RE OUT OF LUCK WITHOUT GLUE

RALPHIE.
SO ... TRY AGAIN

RANDY.
NOTHING FITS

RALPHIE.
THIS MIGHT WORK

RANDY.
CALL IT QUITS
WHAT'S THE POINT?

RALPHIE.
JUST DO THE BEST WE CAN

RALPHIE & RANDY.
BEFORE THE OLD MAN COMES HOME

RALPHIE. And there oughta be something we can do to make Mom feel better.

RANDY. Like what?

RALPHIE. Well, for one thing, *you* could start eating your food without all that little piggy stuff.

RANDY *(disinclined)*. Aawwww ...

(The BOYS go to the kitchen table, where RALPHIE tries to coax RANDY into eating some of his dinner.)

RALPHIE.
> SHE'LL COME BACK
> SEE YOUR PLATE
> WON'T BELIEVE THAT YOU ATE
> TRY TO SWALLOW JUST ONE CARROT

RANDY.
> I DON'T KNOW IF I CAN

RALPHIE *(imploring him)*.
> OPEN UP, BE A MAN

RANDY.
> IT'S TOO MUCH

RALPHIE.
> THEN FINE, WE'LL SHARE IT
> HEY, IF YOU JUST TAKE A BITE
> THEY WON'T REMEMBER THEIR FIGHT

RANDY .
> ALL RIGHT.
> *(He reluctantly takes a bite.)*

RALPHIE.
> FORCE IT DOWN
> REALLY QUICK

RANDY *(mouth full, unable to swallow)*.
> I THINK I'M …
> GETTING SICK

RALPHIE.
> THIS COULD WORK!

RANDY *(again, giving up).*
     WE NEED A BETTER PLAN

RALPHIE & RANDY.
     BEFORE THE OLD MAN COMES HOME

     IF HE SEES THAT THE LAMP IS ON
     IF SHE SEES THAT THE FOOD IS GONE
     MAYBE THEN THAT'S WHEN
     EVERYTHING WILL BE OK AGAIN

(THE OLD MAN enters, carrying a paper bag. RALPHIE and RANDY quickly creep out of his way. THE OLD MAN takes out a bottle of glue and kneels beside the lamp in semi-darkness and begins to work on it.)

JEAN. The Old Man returned later with five bottles of extra-strength glue. He worked furiously but futilely for at least an hour. At last, he gave in to the inevitability that the precious leg was lost. Not long afterward, Mother returned.

(MOTHER enters. RALPHIE and RANDY look relieved, but they are still anxious. THE OLD MAN looks up and sees MOTHER, who crosses slowly to him. They look at each other for a moment. They try to express themselves as best they can, speak-singing, neither exactly capable of doing so nor wanting to completely surrender. They communicate in sentence fragments.)

MOTHER. Frank …
     LOOK, I JUST …

THE OLD MAN.
     IF I WAS …

MOTHER.
     WHAT I MEANT …

THE OLD MAN.
IT'S BECAUSE …

MOTHER.
HOW ON EARTH …

THE OLD MAN & MOTHER.
IT GOT THIS WAY

MOTHER.
WHEN I SAID …

THE OLD MAN.
I WAS SO …

MOTHER *(earnestly)*.
AND I TRIED …

THE OLD MAN *(understanding)*.
YEAH, I KNOW …

MOTHER.
LISTEN, FRANK, WHAT I MEAN TO SAY …
(Whispering.) I'm sorry.

(MOTHER holds her hand out to THE OLD MAN, which he takes.)

THE OLD MAN *(whimpering, child-like)*. Look at it.

(He collapses into her arms. As she cradles him, she waves RALPHIE and RANDY away, who return to their room upstairs.)

JEAN *(with great relief)*. The white flag had been waved. The war was over. Peace had once again returned to the land.

(THE OLD MAN picks up the pieces of the lamp and slowly begins to exit.)

JEAN *(cont'd)*. With as much dignity as he could muster, the old man took what was left of his major award out into the backyard and buried it next to the garage.

(THE OLD MAN has exited the house and is seen outside.)

JEAN *(cont'd, as if recalling a distant memory)*. I could never be sure, but I thought I could hear—

(The first notes of "Taps" are heard. JEAN salutes as the lights on the Parker family house fade. THE OLD MAN exits the stage in a dignified funeral march.)

(#16a: "The Night Before Christmas")

JEAN *(cont'd)*. With the family unit back intact, we all refocused on the day ahead. We knew that Santa and his reindeer had already left the North Pole. And that all good little boys and girls had to be asleep when they arrived. They just had to.

SCENE 7

(RALPHIE and RANDY's bedroom. A half hour or so later.)

MOTHER *(peeking into the boys' bedroom)*. It's nine o'clock, boys. You gotta get to sleep. Santa's on his way. *(She exits.)*

(RALPHIE and RANDY lie in bed, both a bit restless.)

(#17: "Somewhere Hovering Over Indiana")

RANDY. Ralphie, are you asleep?
RALPHIE. No … Are you?

(A beat. RANDY determines whether or not he is dreaming).

RANDY. I don't think so …

RALPHIE.
> I TOSS AND TURN
> TURN AND TOSS AGAIN
> HEAR THE CLOCK TICK-A-TOCK
> IT GOES SO SLOW
> LEGS CRISS AND CROSS AGAIN
> COUNT A BILLION SHEEP
> BUT I STILL CAN'T SLEEP

RANDY *(too antsy to sleep, he sits straight up)*.
> RIGHT WHEN I'M GONNA BUST
> FLIP, FLOP AND READJUST

RALPHIE & RANDY.
> CAN'T GO TO BED, INSTEAD MY
> MIND BEGINS TO RACE
> SOMETHING'S TAKING PLACE
>
> EV'RY YEAR I WAIT UP TO HEAR
> HIM GO, "HO, HO, HO," 'CAUSE I KNOW
>
> SOMEWHERE HOVERING OVER INDIANA
> SANTA'S COVERING GROUND WITH LIGHTNING
>   SPEED
>
> HIGH ABOVE THE TOWN
> FLYING DOWN
> BETTER CATCH HIM QUICK
> OLD SAINT NICK

RALPHIE.
> MAYBE STILL IN EVANSVILLE

RANDY.
> OR SOMEWHERE

RALPHIE & RANDY.
> HOVERING OVER INDIANA
> ACROSS THE WHOLE STATE AND STRAIGHT TO ME

(Suddenly, in various parts of the stage, all of the KIDS, in pajamas, appear in their own worlds, unable to sleep.)

KID 1.
>I TRIED REAL HARD TO BE GOOD THIS YEAR

KID 2.
>BUT I MADE A MISTAKE OR TWO

FLICK.
>OR TWELVE

KID 3.
>HE UNDERSTOOD THIS YEAR
>*RIGHT?*

SCHWARTZ.
>WHEN I LOST MY HAT

DILL *(taking slight pleasure in this "mistake").*
>WHEN I KILLED MY CAT

(As the fantasy world of the KIDS materializes, the Parker family house fades away).

ALL KIDS.
>PLEASE LET MY NAME EXIST FAR
>FROM THE NAUGHTY LIST
>
>I WOULD BE TWICE AS NICE IF
>HE WOULD JUST UNPACK
>SOMETHING FROM THE SACK
>
>SOMETHING BETTER THAN
>JUST A SWEATER FOR ME
>WE'LL SEE! HE MIGHT BE
>
>SOMEWHERE HOVERING OVER INDIANA
>SANTA'S COVERING GROUND AND GAINING SPEED
>HIGH ABOVE THE TOWN

FLYING DOWN
ON A REINDEER FLIGHT
THROUGH THE NIGHT

RALPHIE & RANDY.
ZOOMING INTO BLOOMINGTON OR

ALL KIDS.
SOMEWHERE HOVERING OVER INDIANA
INDIANA …
ACROSS THE WHOLE STATE AND STRAIGHT TO ME

(The KIDS imagine Santa's snowy sleigh ride through their town.)

2 KIDS.
HE'LL COME SWERVING DOWN THE HILL

3 KIDS.
CATCH THE CURVE AROUND THE MILL

2 KIDS.
MAYBE SKATE ALONG
THE BRANCHES OF THE TREES

KIDS *(except RALPHIE and RANDY)*.
YOU MIGHT SPOT HIM IN THE FIELDS

KID 1.
CAREFUL NOT TO HIT MISS SHIELDS!

RALPHIE & RANDY.
HURRY THROUGH THE FLURRY
AND, GET HERE, PRETTY PLEASE!

ALL KIDS.
PRETTY PLEASE!!

HE'S SOMEWHERE HOVERING OVER INDIANA
INDIANA

RALPHIE & RANDY.
ACROSS THE WHOLE STATE
ACROSS THE WHOLE STATE

ALL KIDS.
AND STRAIGHT

RALPHIE & RANDY.	KIDS.
TO ME!	SOMEWHERE HOVERING OVER INDIANA
TO ME!	TO ME!

THE OLD MAN *(offstage, startling all the KIDS)*. Boys, stop that cracklin' racket, or I'll tell Santa to fly right over our flim-flammin' house!

(#18: "Christmas Morning")

(The KIDS return to their own worlds, creeping offstage and back to bed to wait for Santa to visit.)

KIDS 1 *(sleepily, dreamily)*.
SOMEWHERE HOVERING OVER INDIANA …

KIDS 2.
SOMEWHERE HOVERING OVER INDIANA …

SCENE 8

(RALPHIE and RANDY get back in bed and sleep for a moment as the sun rises on the Parker family house. Christmas morning. RALPHIE and RANDY awaken with the sunrise. RALPHIE pops out of bed and calls to his brother.)

RALPHIE *(with a start)*.
IT'S CHRISTMAS!
IT'S CHRISTMAS!

RALPHIE & RANDY.
>IT'S CHRISTMAS!
>IT'S CHRISTMAS!
>IT'S CHRISTMAS!
>IT'S CHRISTMAS!
>IT'S CHRISTMAS DAY!

(RALPHIE and RANDY run downstairs, where gifts, most of them wrapped, adorn the living room.)

RALPHIE. Wow!

RANDY. Wow! Look at that!

THE OLD MAN & MOTHER *(entering from upstairs, quite bleary-eyed)*. Merry Christmas!

RANDY. Hey! … Wow, a fire truck! That one's mine! That one's mine!

MOTHER *(to RANDY)*. Wait for Christmas to start, honey.

(MOTHER takes a turkey from the oven in the kitchen and sets it on the counter.)

RANDY. I wanna play Santa! I wanna play Santa.

THE OLD MAN. Wait a minute, you played Santa last year— Ralphie, you play Santa!

(RALPHIE is perfectly content to let RANDY play Santa.)

RANDY. Awww …

THE OLD MAN *(barking)*. Ralphie plays Santa!

RALPHIE *(frightened)*. OK.

RANDY. What's in here?! Oh, it's hard *(Opens the gift.)* A zeppelin! Thank you, Ralphie!

THE OLD MAN *(opening a gift)*. A can of Simoniz. Thank you, Ralphie.

(MOTHER drops a wrapped blue bowling ball into the THE OLD MAN's lap, inches from his crotch.)

MOTHER. From me to you.

THE OLD MAN *(winces, then opens it)*. You gave me a blue ball. *(Briefly pauses.)* A blue bowling ball. Thank you, my dear.

RALPHIE *(picking up a gift, desperate)*.
    THIS HAS TO BE THE BOX
    'CAUSE IT ALL COMES DOWN TO CHRISTMAS

(He unwraps it to find that it's a box of socks. Disappointed.)

    I CAN'T GET STUCK WITH SOCKS
    'CAUSE IT ALL COMES DOWN TO CHRISTMAS

    I'VE GOT ONE SHOT AND IT'S ONLY ONE GIFT AWAY

(He eyes the final, remaining, long box.)

    IT'S GOTTA BE, IT'S GOTTA BE
    IT'S GOTTA BE, IT'S GOTTA BE
    THE GUN ON CHRISTMAS

(He rips off the wrapping, opens the top of the box and stares inside. Horrified, he pulls out a pink bunny suit.)

    NOOOOOO!!!

MOTHER *(loving it)*. Aunt Clara always gives you the nicest things, Ralphie. Go upstairs and put it on.

RALPHIE *(devastated)*. I don't want to.

MOTHER. Go on.

(RALPHIE, still in a state of stunned disbelief, takes the box upstairs and goes into his bedroom.)

THE OLD MAN. Which one's Aunt Clara? The one with the mustache?

MOTHER *(protective)*. She has a slight mustache, yes. She's very nice.

THE OLD MAN. She's not nice to me. I think she used to play linebacker for the Packers.

(THE OLD MAN moves toward the turkey as MOTHER looks upstairs.)

MOTHER. Hurry up, Ralphie!

JEAN. Now, it was known throughout the Midwest that The Old Man was a turkey junkie. A bona fide golly turkacanus freak.

(THE OLD MAN takes a pinch of the turkey and nibbles it. MOTHER notices THE OLD MAN at the turkey.)

MOTHER. Frank! Don't pick at it. You'll get sick! It still needs basting, then back in the oven.

THE OLD MAN. This piece looks cooked. *(Taking a pinch.)* Mmmmm … turkey. *(Delighted.)* Heaven. Turkey!

MOTHER. Frank! Please! *(Calling upstairs to RALPHIE.)* Ralphie, now you come down here and show everybody what Aunt Clara gave you.

RALPHIE *(offstage, from upstairs)*. I don't want to.

MOTHER. Come down here right now and show us that present. She went to all that trouble to make it.

RALPHIE *(insistently pleading)*. Aw, Mom …

MOTHER *(fed up)*. Come down here. COME DOWN HERE! COME DOWN …

(RALPHIE appears in the pink bunny suit at the top of the stairs, then slowly starts to come down, sulking all the way. Meanwhile, THE OLD MAN is pouring wine at the table.)

MOTHER *(cont'd, adoring the childish, girlish costume)*. Ohhhhh … that's so cute.

JEAN *(miffed)*. My Aunt Clara had for years labored under the delusion that I was not only perpetually four years old, but also a *girl*.

MOTHER. That's the most precious thing I've ever seen.

JEAN. If Flick or Schwartz ever saw me in this, my life at school would be a veritable hell.

MOTHER. He looks so sweeeeeeet.

(RANDY giggles.)

RALPHIE *(quickly)*. Shut up, Randy.

THE OLD MAN *(a bit disgusted)*. He looks like a deranged Easter bunny.

MOTHER. He does not.

THE OLD MAN. He does, too. He looks like a pink nightmare. Are you happy wearing that?

(RALPHIE shakes his head "no.")

THE OLD MAN *(cont'd)*. You wanna take it off?

(RALPHIE nods emphatically. THE OLD MAN turns to MOTHER.)

THE OLD MAN *(cont'd)*. Come on, tell the kid to take it off.

MOTHER *(concedes)*. All right, you'll only wear it when Aunt Clara visits. Go on and take it off.

(RALPHIE takes off the bunny suit and sits next to THE OLD MAN, who takes a sip of wine.)

THE OLD MAN. You know this wine's not bad … *(Candidly.)* It isn't good either. You want a sip?

RALPHIE *(taking the glass)*. Yep.

MOTHER *(snatching the glass from RALPHIE)*. No, you don't …

(RALPHIE goes and sits near the tree. Disappointed, he mindlessly fiddles with a new football he has received.)

MOTHER *(cont')*. Did you have a nice Christmas, Ralph?

RALPHIE *(showing his disappointment a bit)*. Yeah. Pretty nice.

THE OLD MAN. Yeah? … Did you get everything you wanted?

RALPHIE. Uhn … almost.

THE OLD MAN. Almost, huh? *(Weary and blunt.)* Well … that's life. *(Takes a gulp of wine.)* There's always next Christmas … *(A beat. Then, he feigns a bit of surprise as he questions RALPHIE.)* Hey, what's that over there?

RALPHIE. Where?

THE OLD MAN *(continuing the act)*. Right over there. Right behind the counter. I think I see something. Better go check it out.

(#18a: "Ralphie to the Rescue" [Reprise])

(RALPHIE holds his breath as he crosses to behind the counter and pulls out a long, rectangular wrapped box.)

MOTHER *(asking genuinely, privately)*. What is it, Frank?

(RALPHIE rips off the wrapping and tears open the box within. He excitedly opens the gift as THE OLD MAN beams with delight, and MOTHER laughs under her breath. RAL-PHIE withdraws the air rifle from the box.)

RALPHIE *(reading the label on the box, in delirious ecstasy)*.
AN OFFICIAL RED RYDER RANGE MODEL
CARBINE-ACTION BB GUN!

ENSEMBLE *(except THE PARKERS, and out of nowhere)*.
AHHHHHH!

RALPHIE *(in absolute heaven)*.
WITH A COMPASS IN THE STOCK
AND THIS THING THAT TELLS TIME!

(The ENSEMBLE disappears).

MOTHER. Who put it there?

THE OLD MAN *(quickly)*. Santa Claus. *(Assuring her.)* I had one when I was his age.

ENSEMBLE.
   AHHHHHH!

JEAN. Oh, it was beautiful. I could hardly wait to try it out.

THE OLD MAN *(pulling a small cylinder of BBs from his pocket)*. Come on, I'll show you how to load it. *(Loading the gun as RALPHIE continues to adore it, in shock.)* Gotta make sure none of the BB's fall on the floor.

RALPHIE. Can—can I try it out, Mom? Can I?

MOTHER. OK. But be careful … I still say those things are dangerous.

   (She calls out to RALPHIE as he goes outside.)

MOTHER *(cont'd)*. Don't shoot any birds or animals!

THE OLD MAN. Except the Bumpus hounds!

   (The scene shifts to outside of the Parker family house. The PRAIRIE ENSEMBLE appears to celebrate the victory with RALPHIE.)

PRAIRIE ENSEMBLE.
   RALPHIE TO THE RESCUE!

RALPHIE.
   OH!

PRAIRIE ENSEMBLE.
   OH!
   RALPHIE TO THE RESCUE!

RALPHIE & PRAIRIE ENSEMBLE.
   OH!

PRAIRIE ENSEMBLE.
>   FIRIN' FAST
>   HE'S A COWBOY AT LAST
>   NOW LET HER BLOW
>   BLOW
>   BLOW!

(PRAIRIE ENSEMBLE exits.)

RALPHIE *(as Red Ryder)*. OK, Black Bart. Now you get yours.

(RALPHIE aims at a target and shoots the gun. We hear pinging sounds, followed by tinkling glass. RALPHIE drops the gun and quickly puts his hand up to his face, knocking his glasses off. JEAN enters in horror.)

JEAN. Oh my God, I shot my eye out!

MOTHER *(calling out the back door)*. Ralphie, you be careful out there. Don't shoot your eye out.

JEAN. She hadn't seen! She didn't know!

(RALPHIE uncovers his face and blinks a few times.)

JEAN *(cont'd)*. My eye's all right. The BB must have hit my glasses … my glasses! Oh, no!

(RALPHIE blindly searches for his glasses.)

JEAN *(cont'd)*. Where are my glasses? Few things brought such swift and terrible retribution on a kid as a pair of busted glasses!

(RALPHIE accidentally steps on his glasses. A crunching sound is heard.)

JEAN *(cont'd)*. Oh, no.

RALPHIE. Oh, no.

JEAN. Oh, no, pulverized.

(RALPHIE picks up the mangled glasses.)

MOTHER *(from inside the house)*. Frank, stay away from that turkey. You'll get worms. Where's Ralphie?

JEAN. Rapidly my mind evolved a spectacular plot … It had to work. Quickly, I whipped up some tears.

(RALPHIE whimpers as MOTHER enters the yard.)

RALPHIE *(a tear-filled yelp, putting on a show)*. Mommy!

MOTHER. Ralphie? What's the matter, baby? What happened? *(Examines his face.)*

RALPHIE *(crying)*. There was … this … *(Improvising.)* icicle!

MOTHER. Icicle?

RALPHIE *(weepy and dramatic)*. Yeah, an icicle, and it fell off the garage roof and hit my cheek, and it broke my glasses … and I tried to get out of the way … but I couldn't …

MOTHER. Ah, lemme see. It's just a little bump. You poor thing! You're lucky it didn't hit your eye! *(A bit daffy.)* Those icicles have been known to kill people!

RALPHIE. But what about my glasses?

MOTHER *(picking up the glasses)*. Well, you can wear the old ones with the crack in them until we can get you some new ones.

(They start back inside.)

JEAN *(in delirious joy)*. I had pulled it off!

(#18b: "Bumpus Hounds")

(RALPHIE looks out at the audience and smiles, then immediately resumes crying to his MOTHER. They exit.)

JEAN *(cont'd)*. It had worked! Victory was mine! Ah, life is like that. Sometimes at the height of our reveries, when our joy is at its zenith, when all is most right with the world—the most unthinkable disasters descend upon us.

(Low barking and growling sounds are heard, with music corresponding, as the BUMPUS HOUNDS enter the house through the open door, left ajar by MOTHER. In a well-choreographed sequence, they chase down THE OLD MAN, who loses control of and spills the turkey and fillings. The BUMPUS HOUNDS devour THE OLD MAN's precious bird. He is grumbling, screaming throughout.

Note: If real dogs are not used for the BUMPUS HOUNDS, unseen actors behind the table holding the turkey may wave prop dog tails and make barking sounds while pulling the pan of turkey behind the table and tossing pieces of turkey into the air.)

THE OLD MAN. What the—? Shoo! Git! Scort! Bumpus!

(The BUMPUS HOUNDS exit as MOTHER and RALPHIE enter to see what has happened, in horror.)

THE OLD MAN *(cont'd, in disbelief, completely losing it).* The Bumpus … the hounds … the door … You left the back door open!

MOTHER. Oh, no!

THE OLD MAN *(his most epic faux-swearing bout yet).* Son's britches! *(Defeated, he whimpers.)* Bumpus!

(They all stand in horror at the turkey carnage. THE OLD MAN is livid. MOTHER is devastated. RALPHIE and RANDY are in shock.)

JEAN *(as ALL dejectedly examine the turkey remains).* The heavenly aroma still hung heavy in the house. But it was gone—all gone. No turkey, no turkey sandwiches, no turkey salad, no turkey hash, no turkey nothin'. Gone. All gone.

(After a long pause, THE OLD MAN accepts what has happened and attempts to save their Christmas dinner.)

THE OLD MAN. All right … Let's get our coats. We are going out to eat.

(A gong sounds.)

(#18c: "To the Chop Suey Palace")

JEAN. Now there was only one place that might possibly be open on Christmas Day in Hohman, Indiana. A place we'd never been to before … We were in luck.

(THE PARKERS arrive at a traditional Chinese restaurant, the Chop Suey Palace.)

WAITER. Table for four?
THE OLD MAN. Uh … yeah.

(The WAITER seats THE PARKERS at a table. He hands out menus and sets a pot of tea on the table. He is assisted by his daughter. WAITER'S DAUGHTER is a waiter-in-training.)

THE OLD MAN *(cont'd)*. Do you have turkey?
WAITER *(matter-of-fact)*. Duck.
THE OLD MAN. Duck?
WAITER. Tastes just like turkey.
THE OLD MAN. All right. Duck.

(The WAITER and WAITER'S DAUGHTER go to retrieve the food.)

RALPHIE. Where are all the people, Dad?
MOTHER. At home with their families.
THE OLD MAN. Oh, look, there are the Schwartzes.

(They wave to their good friends, unseen across the restaurant. The WAITER approaches the table with a full duck on

a platter as the WAITER'S DAUGHTER sets two or three bowls of food on the table. THE PARKERS are taken aback at the sight of the full duck lying on the platter.)

MOTHER *(looking skeptically at the duck)*. It's … it's …

THE OLD MAN. Yes, it's a beautiful duck, it really is, but you see, *(Gesturing to the head, still attached.)* it's smiling at me.

(The WAITER swiftly chops off the head of the duck and puts it in his pocket. THE PARKERS react accordingly.)

WAITER. And now I sing American Christmas song for you. Like Bing Crosby. *(He sings with a thick accent).*
    DECK THE HALL WITH BOUGH OF HOLLY
    FA RA RA RA RA RA RA RA RA RA
    'TIS THE SEASON TO BE JOLLY
    FA RA RA RA RA RA RA RA RA RA

(The WAITER gestures for the family to join in.)

THE PARKERS & WAITER.
    DON WE NOW OUR GAY APPAREL
    FA LA LA LA LA LA LA LA LA LA
    TROLL THE ANCIENT YULETIDE CAROL
    FA LA LA LA LA LA LA LA LA LA

(The WAITER pours a glass of plum wine for THE OLD MAN, MOTHER and himself. They rise to toast the occasion. THE OLD MAN and MOTHER take a gulp and react—a bit stronger than expected.)

WAITER. Yeah, pack a punch. Sit! Eat!

(JEAN speaks as the food is spooned onto individual dishes.)

JEAN. That Christmas would live in our memories as the Christmas when we were introduced to Chinese turkey.

(#19: "A Christmas Story")

(THE PARKERS consider the craziness of this particular holiday season. As they eat, they sing with sweetness but also humor. Not saccharine or overly-sentimental. They are happy to be together and aware of the irony in eating Chinese food for Christmas dinner.)

THE OLD MAN.
>WHAT A PERFECT SCENE
>ON A CHRISTMAS NIGHT
>SO WE MIGHT BE STUCK WITH DUCK
>BUT THE WORLD'S ALL RIGHT

MOTHER.
>AND YOU HAVE TO LAUGH
>IT'S A GIANT MESS
>BUT IF NO ONE CRIED

THE OLD MAN.
>OR DIED

THE OLD MAN & MOTHER.
>IT'S A BIG SUCCESS

THE OLD MAN *(with relief)*. Right?
MOTHER. Right.
>THIS YEAR WE NEARLY WENT INSANE

THE OLD MAN.
>THIS YEAR WE GAVE UP STUFFING FOR CHOW MEIN

RANDY *(eating voluntarily for the first time in a long while)*. This is good!
MOTHER *(incredulous, stunned at RANDY's surprising love of Chinese food)*. Of course.

THE OLD MAN.
>WHAT A CHRISTMAS STORY TO BEHOLD
A CRAZY CHRISTMAS STORY TO BE TOLD
WE GOT A BIRD WITH NO HEAD
A POT FULLA TEA

MOTHER.
>WHAT'S TO BE SAID
WHEN YOU ARE HERE NEXT TO ME?

THE OLD MAN *(softening just a bit)*. Yeah …

THE OLD MAN & MOTHER.
>WHO COULD WANT MUCH MORE?
OUR CHRISTMAS STORY

(The family continues eating their meal, sharing dishes.)

RALPHIE.
>I HAD ONE BIG WISH

THE OLD MAN.
>SANTA SOMEHOW KNEW

RALPHIE.
>RIGHT BEFORE MY EYES

MOTHER.
>SURPRISE!

RALPHIE.
>MY WISH CAME TRUE

MOTHER.
>THIS YEAR WE MIGHT NOT HAVE A LOT

THE OLD MAN.
>THIS YEAR I'LL TELL YA ONE THING THAT WE'VE GOT

(They have finished their meal. They pay their bill, gather their coats and head outside as snow falls.)

THE OLD MAN & MOTHER.
> WHAT A CHRISTMAS STORY TO BEHOLD

THE PARKERS.
> A CRAZY CHRISTMAS STORY TO BE TOLD

THE OLD MAN.
> I'LL TAKE THE CHEAP CHRISTMAS WINES

MOTHER.
> THE SLUSH IN THE STREET

THE OLD MAN & MOTHER.
> THE CROWDS AND THE LINES
> THAT MAKE THE SEASON COMPLETE

THE PARKERS.
> WHO COULD ASK FOR MORE?
> THIS CHRISTMAS STORY

(Families from the town enter and gather around. We see them in various settings, each forming their own family unit. JEAN is at the center of this, basking in the warmth of the moment and recalling, perhaps even envisioning, the many quirky and lovely memories he has of this special Christmas, his family and this time in his young life.)

ALL.
> YEARS MAY PASS BUT
> STILL WE WILL REMEMBER

GROUP 1.
> WONDER WHERE WE'LL BE

GROUP 2.
> BEING HERE TOGETHER THIS DECEMBER

GROUP 1.
  ALL AROUND OUR TREE

ALL.
  SEEING EV'RY GIRL AND BOY
  WITH A HEART SO FULL OF

GROUP 1.
  JOY.

GROUP 2.
  WE'LL LOOK BACK SOMEDAY

GROUP 1.
  FROM FAR AWAY

ALL *(except KIDS)*.
  WE'LL SAY:

ALL *(except TENOR 1)*.	TENOR 1.
WHAT A CHRISTMAS STORY TO BEHOLD	AH
	WHAT A CHRISTMAS STORY TO
A CRAZY CHRISTMAS STORY TO BE TOLD	BEHOLD TO BE TOLD

(All except JEAN exit. The scene gradually shifts back to the Parker family house. MOTHER and THE OLD MAN put RALPHIE and RANDY to bed.)

JEAN *(softly, but still buoyant)*. Back in those days you never asked yourself, "Do my parents love me?" It never crossed your mind. You were there. They took care of you. Their job was to raise you. Your job was to let them. When they said, "Don't run with scissors," or "Button your coat," or … "You'll shoot your eye out," maybe even *they* didn't know it—but that's what it was … love …

(A beat.)

JEAN *(cont'd)*. That night, next to me in the darkness lay my cold, blue, steel beauty—the greatest gift I had ever received. Are you kiddin'? *(Attempting to control his emotions.)* My old man, my *dad*, gave it to me. That's why it was the greatest gift I would *ever* receive. *(After a moment, he returns to his usual narrative demeanor.)* As the excitement of the day gradually subsided, I finally drifted off to sleep, pranging ducks on the wing and getting off spectacular hip shots.

(THE OLD MAN and MOTHER have come back downstairs and are alone, perhaps sitting together by the tree.)

MOTHER.
 CHRISTMAS IS HERE
 THIS CALM, QUIET NIGHT

THE OLD MAN.
 IT COMES ONCE A YEAR

THE OLD MAN & MOTHER.
 SO YOU HOLD ON TO IT TIGHT
 WHO COULD WANT MUCH MORE?
 A CHRISTMAS STORY

(JEAN's radio studio has materialized one final time. He thoughtfully finishes his broadcast.)

JEAN *(looking toward RALPHIE's bedroom)*. Good night, Ralphie. *(To the audience.)* Good night all. Thanks for listening. Merry Christmas.

(If used at the beginning, the "On Air" sign goes out.)

END OF ACT II

(#20: "Bows")

(All enter, in turn, for bows.)

THE OLD MAN, MOTHER, MEN & WOMEN.
   RALPHIE TO THE RESCUE!

KIDS.
   OH

THE OLD MAN, MOTHER, MEN & WOMEN.
   OH!

ALL.
   RALPHIE TO THE RESCUE!
   OH!

   A BOY AND HIS GUN
   RIDING OFF IN THE SUN
   JUST WATCH HIM GO!
   GO!
   GO!

   YIPPEE-KAY-O!

*(The BUMPUS HOUNDS take their bow in grand fashion,
chasing THE OLD MAN across the stage one final time.)*

(#21: "Exit Music")

NOTES

NOTES